Lessons from the Old Testament

By Dorothy Tatum

Lessons from the Old Testament is copyright © Dorothy Tatum, 2017. All rights reserved.

Published in the United States of America by:
Cobb Publishing
704 E. Main St
Charleston, AR 72933
(479) 747-8372
CobbPublishing@gmail.com
www.CobbPublishing.com

978-1-947622-06-7

Dear Student:

    It's good to have you in our Bible class. We hope you will want to be here each Sunday to learn and grow in God's word. To get the most from our study, regular attendance is very important.

    During this session, we will be studying from the Old Testament. Even though some of the stories are familiar to you, we will study them in a different way than when you were at a younger age. Our plan is to grow our knowledge of God's Word.

    We want our study to be fun as well as informative. We want you to participate with your ideas also, just remember that courtesy to each other is a Christian virtue.

    Before class time, please study your lesson; bring your notebook and Bible to class each week, and be on time... these things will help you to learn more during our class time.

    It would be fun if you learned your memory verse every week to answer roll call. Try to do this—it will be fun and a challenge!

    If you have any questions, ask your teacher for help.

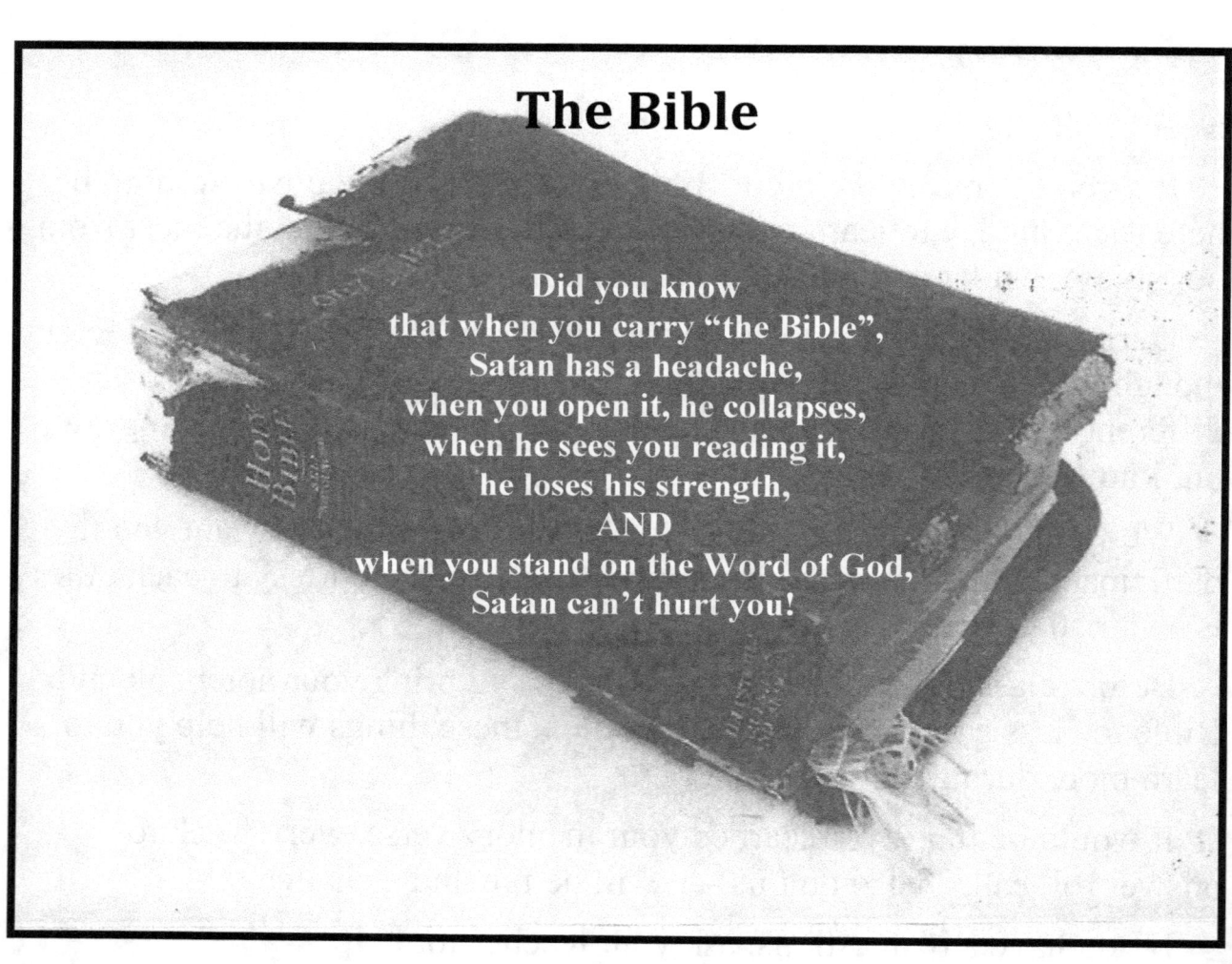

The Bible

Did you know
that when you carry "the Bible",
Satan has a headache,
when you open it, he collapses,
when he sees you reading it,
he loses his strength,
AND
when you stand on the Word of God,
Satan can't hurt you!

Facts About The Bible...
THE BIBLE IS A COLLECTION OF 66 BOOKS...
WRITTEN BY 40 DIFFERENT MEN...
OVER A PERIOD OF APPROXIMATELY 1500-1600 YEARS.

Old Testament (39 books, four sections)

Law	*History*	*Poetry*	*Prophecy*
Genesis Exodus Leviticus Numbers Deuteronomy	Joshua Judges Ruth 1 & 2 Samuel 1 & 2 Kings 1 & 2 Chronicles Ezra Nehemiah Esther	Job Psalms Proverbs Ecclesiastes Song of Solomon	Isaiah Jeremiah Lamentations Ezekiel Daniel Hosea Joel Amos Obadiah Jonah Micah Nahum Habakkuk Zephaniah Haggai Zechariah Malachi

New Testament (27 books, four sections)

Gospels	*History*	*Letters*	*Prophecy*
Matthew Mark Luke John	Acts	Romans 1 & 2 Corinthians Galatians Ephesians Philippians Colossians 1 & 2 Thessalonians 1 & 2 Timothy Titus Philemon Hebrews James 1 & 2 Peter 1, 2 & 3 John Jude	Revelation

BIBLE FACTS I SHOULD LEARN

TESTAMENT means COVENANT or AGREEMENT.

GOD made a COVENANT at Mt. Sinai with the Jewish people. (Law of Moses)

OLD TESTAMENT—39 Books, 32 Writers

The Old Testament gives History of man from creation to 400 years before Christ.

There are FIVE divisions in the Old Testament:

Law (Pentateuch), History, Poetry, Major Prophets, Minor Prophets.

NEW TESTAMENT—27 Books, 8 Writers:

Matthew, Mark, Luke, John, Paul, Peter James, Jude.

The New Testament Is Gods covenant with man who serve Him through Christ. There are FOUR divisions in the New Testament:

- <u>Biography</u> (Christ's birth, life, death, resurrection),
- <u>History</u> of early church (Church established, Acts 2, early growth of church.),
- <u>Letters</u> to People and Churches (Instruction for living Christian life.),
- <u>Prophecy</u>.

GOSPEL—Good news of JESUS CHRIST

_____ _____ _____ _____ _____

TO UNDERSTAND THE BIBLE, WE SHOULD KNOW THAT IT INCLUDES 3 AGES.

Patriarchal Age		**Mosaic Age**		**Christian Age**
2500 year period	R	1500 year period	T	Day of Pentecost, 'til...
	E		H	
God gave instructions to heads of families.	D	Also called the Jewish age. Laws given to Moses at Mt. Sinai	E	God's laws for us through Christ
Some important people of this time:	S E A	Some important people of this time:	C R O S S	Some important people of this time:
Adam		Moses		Christ
Noah		Joshua		Matthew
Abraham		Saul		Peter
Isaac		David		Paul
Jacob		Solomon		Timothy
Joseph		Daniel		Barnabas
		Isaiah		
		Jeremiah*		

*Prophesied that God would make a New Covenant.

BIBLE FACTS I SHOULD KNOW:

1. Three ages: Patriarchal — Mosaic — Christian
2. 27 books in the New Testament: 39 books in the Old Testament; 66 books Total.
3. 1189 Chapters in the Bible.
4. It took about 1600 years to whit- Bible.
5. 8 men wrote the New Testament.
6. 40 men wrote the Bible.
7. Psalms 117 is shortest chapter in the Bible. Psalms 119 is the longest chapter in the Bible.
8. Bible written in these languages: Hebrew, Aramaic, Greek.
9. Purpose of the Bible: To tell man of Jesus saving power.
10. Theme of Bible: Redemption of man.
11. Moses wrote Genesis.
12. John wrote Revelations.
13. Book of Acts: History of Church.
14. Inspiration of Bible: God breathed.
15. Moses wrote first 5 books of Bible—called the Pentateuch (Law)
16. Joint wrote 5 books—John, 1, 2, 3 John, and Revelation.
17. Shortest verse in the Bible is John 11:35.
18. The second coming of Christ is mentioned in every book of the New Testament' except Philemon
19. God's name does not appear in the Book of Esther.
20. The only woman whose age appears in the Bible is Sarah, Abraham's wife.

THE BOOKS OF LAW
(THE PENTATEUCH)

Genesis 1

GOD'S WONDERFUL WORLD

A Story About Orderliness

MEMORY VERSE: Genesis 1:1

In the beginning, there was nothing— nothing but God. No world had been made, no sun, moon or stars. There were no birds or animals or plants or trees. Instead, there was nothing but darkness and empty space.

But God had a wonderful plan. He called it creation. God would fill the dark empty spaces with beautiful things. He would make these beautiful things from nothing.

At the right time, God began His wonderful work. "Let there be light!" God said. Light appeared in the dark skies and the darkness hid from it. God called the light places day and the dark places night.

"Let there be a sky above and an earth below!" God said. The earth formed into a beautiful ball and the sky rose above it. A clear horizon appeared where the earth and the sky met.

"Let the waters gather together and the dry land appear," God said. The waters moved together to form the seas and the dry land appeared, with mountains and valleys and fields.

"Let grass and plants and trees grow upon the dry land," God said. The land burst forth with beautiful flowers and bushes, trees and plants. God must have smiled at the wonder of it all.

God spoke and the sun warmed the earth. He spoke and the moon appeared. One by one stars twinkled in the skies.

"Let birds and fish and animals appear," God said. The quiet skies broke forth in birdsong and the still waters sparkled with fish. Animals ran across the hills. The earth was a garden of beauty and harmony. Everything was exactly where it should be, and everything worked together exactly the way it should, like the parts of a beautiful watch. And God saw that it was good!

Genesis, Chapter 1

1. In what verse does God say "Let there be light?" _____
2. Verse 5 speaks of light and darkness. Light is _____ and darkness is _____. This happened on the _____ day.
3. In verse 8 God speaks of the firmament He created. He called it _____. This was the _____ day.
4. Read verses 9-13. On the third day, God made the _____, _____, and growing things; _____ and _____.
5. God created lights. Read verse 14-19. The lights were the _____, _____ and _____. This was done on the _____ day.
6. Verse 21 tells us God created _____ for the sea and _____ for the sky. This was day _____. (vs. 23)
7. Read verses 25-31. God created several more things on the sixth day. From the verses you have read, name the things God made. _____
   _____
8. As God created different things on different days He would make a statement. Can you find it in verse 10, verse 12, verse 18 and verse 31? What was the statement? _____

Think about the world that God made. The world keeps better time in its movement than the finest watch. Think about the beautiful flowers that come from seed.

From this story you learn about God's orderliness. God put everything in the right place. When the world gets out of place, it is because we messed it up... God didn't.

The book of Genesis was written by _____.

10

Genesis 2

THE FIRST HOME
A Story About Happiness

MEMORY VERSE: Genesis 2:24

The whole earth was a beautiful garden, with sights and sounds and smells blending together. God was pleased with His work. He was pleased to see how well everything worked together. But it was too wonderful to keep for Himself alone. God planned to share it with someone—someone like Himself.

One place was more beautiful than all others. God created a man, named him Adam, and put him in charge of this beautiful garden called Eden.

One day God brought each kind of animal to Adam so that he could name them. Then He put Adam in charge of the animals. Adam was glad for the animals, but something—someone—was missing. God knew who this someone was, and He knew what to do.

God put Adam to sleep and then took a rib from his side and made a woman. He brought the woman to Adam to become his wife. Together Adam and his wife lived happily in Eden. Why shouldn't they be happy? What more could they need?

Adam and Eve not only had everything they needed, but they also had everything they wanted. Then God told them about something they could not have, something they should not want.

"You may eat anything in the Garden of Eden except one fruit," God told them. "If you eat the fruit from the tree of the knowledge of good and evil you will die."

Adam and Eve listened carefully to God. As long as they obeyed Him, they lived happily in their garden home.

GENESIS, Chapter 2

1. Last week we studied about God's creation which was accomplished in 6 days. We know the week has 7 days, let's see about day 7. Read vs. 2 and 3 and write about it. _____ _____

2. Read verses 4-6. After God created the plants, herbs and trees, etc., how were they watered? _____

3. On the sixth day God created the animals and man. Verse 7 tells us God formed man of the _____ of the _____ and breathed into him the _____ of life.

Read verse 7 in a King James version of the Bible. It states that man became a _____ _____. The animals God created and the man God created were different after they could breathe and move. God gave man a soul that would live forever.

4. God created a beautiful Garden in _____(vs. 8) and it was watered by a _____. (vs. 10)

5. Verse 15 tells us that God put _____ into the garden to tend and keep it. He could use things that grew in the garden for food... except, for one thing. What was that? (vs. 17) _____ What happened if he ate from it? _____

6. All of the animals and birds God created were brought to _____, to see what he would call them (vs. 19-20), so Adam named the _____, the _____ of the air and every _____.

7. Verse 18 tells us Adam was lonely, because he was alone. He needed someone like himself to talk and share with. God said he would make him a _____. In verse 21 He put Adam to _____ and did a sort of operation. He removed a _____ and closed the _____. Verse 22 tells us from this rib God made a _____.

8. <u>Read verse 24</u>. This is still the way God intends for man and woman to be. Adam and his helper (wife) were to be together always. Chapter 3:20 tells us Adam named his wife _____.

From this story you learn about happiness. As long as Adam and Eve obeyed God, they were happy. As long as you obey God and your parents, you can be happy.

We will learn through our study of all the Bible that God expects us to be obedient to His will.

Genesis 3

ADAM and EVE... And Disobedience
A Story About Temptation

MEMORY VERSE: Genesis 3:20

Reread Genesis 2:17. "Did God REALLY say that?" the serpent ask Eve. "God said we may eat anything in the garden except this fruit," Eve answered. "If we eat this, we will die."

"When you eat this fruit, you will see things you never saw before. You will know the difference between good and evil," the serpent Satan said, "You won't die."

When Satan tempts, he tells little half-truths. He was half right and half wrong. Adam and Eve would not immediately die and be buried. But when they' disobeyed God sin would come between them and God. This kind of death is worse than the other.

Eve listened to Satan's words. She thought they were all true. So she ate some of the fruit and gave some to Adam to eat too.

Satan's half-truth was right. Adam and Eve did not lie down and die. They knew they had sinned against God. They knew that sin had come between them and God. They were ashamed, so ashamed that they made fig-leaf clothes to wear and hid from God. They did not want to see God or talk with Him. But God found them and spoke to them.

"Because you did not obey Me, you must leave the Garden of Eden," God told Adam and Eve. "You must work hard for a living. You will have sorrow and pain."

Adam and Eve were sorry now that they had disobeyed God and had sinned.

GENESIS, Chapter 3

1. Verse 1 says the serpent (Satan) was more _____ than any beast of the field.
2. Find the verse that tells us God said not to eat of the fruit of a certain tree. _____ (Look in the first 5 verses.)
3. Eve found the fruit enticing. In verse 6 it says it was _____, _____; _____ and _____ _____.
4. After eating the forbidden fruit Adam and Eve's eyes were _____; they knew they were _____; and sewed clothes of _____ _____ _____. (vs 7)

5. In verse 8-11, as God walked in the Garden, Adam _____ because he was afraid. He said he was _____ and God ask him two questions, what did He ask him?

   a. _____
   b. _____

6. In verse 14, whom did God curse because of this disobedience? _____

7. Then God made Adam and Eve do what? (verse 23) _____

8. In verse 16 God tells Eve, because of her disobedience (sin), she would have _____ when she had _____.

9. In verse 17 & 18, God tells Adam, because of his disobedience (sin) he would _____ the ground where he grew his food. There would be t_____ and t_____ to make his job of growing food harder.

10. Verse 20 explains what Eve's name means. Write the meaning. _____
_____ (This is also your memory verse, be sure to learn it.)

11. Verse 24. Something was put in the way to guard the tree of life. What was it? _____
_____

Satan, the serpent, told Adam and Eve they would not die. Sin separates us from God and without forgiveness we will be eternally lost from God and Heaven. Why do you suppose Adam and Eve ate the forbidden fruit when they already had all they needed?

From this story we learn that God means what he says. If he says to do something, he expects us to do it and if He says do <u>not</u> do something, He means that also. God gives us everything we need for a good life. When we are tempted to do wrong things (sin) we can pray for God to help us

Genesis 4

ADAM'S SONS: CAIN and ABEL

A Story About Jealousy

MEMORY VERSE: Genesis 4:13

After a time, Adam and Eve had a family. They had two sons; one was called Cain and he became a farmer, the other was a shepherd named Abel.

Both sons gave offerings to God. Their offerings were quite different. Abel gave a pleasing gift to God, but Cain did not.

God rewarded Abel more than Cain because of the offerings. He was more pleased with what Abel did and how he lived. Cain did not like this, he became very jealous.

Jealousy can cause us to do bad things. It takes the smile from our faces and laughter and joy from our hearts. This happened to Cain. He became bitter and angry in his heart.

God had let it be known what kind of offerings He would accept, would be pleased with. Abel obeyed and Cain did not. If we do not obey God, it is sin. Cain did not offer the proper gift to God and he sinned.

One day, Cain and Abel were working in the field together. Cain, due to his jealousy, became so angry he struck his brother Abel and killed him. God punished Cain by sending him away from his home and family and from God Himself. Cain ran and ran...he was lonely and afraid but kept on running. His jealousy had caused him to do a terrible thing.

Genesis 4

1. Verse 1 & 2. Which of Adam's sons was the older? _____
2. The son's occupation were: _____ Cain was a _____ and Abel was a _____
3. Verse 3 & 4. What type of offering did the two sons of Adam bring to the Lord? Cain _____ Abel _____
4.
5. In what verse do we see that God was displeased with Cain's offering? (Look in verses 4-7) _____
6. How did God feel about Abel's offering? (vs. 4) _____
7. Verse 6 & 7. God said to Cain "Why are you _____? If you do

_____ you will be accepted. If you do not do well _____ lies at the door."

8. In verse 8 we read that Cain killed his brother Abel. In verse 9 God ask Cain, "Where is Abel, your brother?" Cain's reply was "Am I my brother's _____?" In other words, "I don't have to keep up with him, or care about him."

9. What did God see on the ground that made him know Abel was dead? _____ (vs.10)

10. God placed a curse on Cain. Cain was a farmer but in verse 12 God says it would no longer _____ it's _____ to him.

11. Cain's reply is your memory verse. Write it here and memorize it._____
_____
_____

12. We read in verse 14 that Cain was a fugitive and a _____ and was afraid someone would _____ him.

13. But, God told Cain that no one would kill him and he set a _____ on Cain. (vs . 15)

We learn from this story what terrible things jealousy can cause us to do. We should guard against becoming jealous of a friend or neighbor or anyone. We should be happy when others can do well, are successful and happy. Prayers to God can help us overcome jealousy and help us to be strong enough to avoid this sin.

PRAY OFTEN

Genesis 6 & 7

NOAH And The FLOOD
A Story of Obedience

MEMORY VERSE: Genesis 6:6

Many years passed after the time of Cain and Abel. People forgot about God and lived the way they wanted to live, not the way God wanted them to live. By the time of Noah, almost everyone was living sad, sinful lives. Only Noah and his family pleased God.

God was not pleased with Noah's wicked neighbors. He was sorry that He had made them. So God said, "I will destroy these people and their animals." Only Noah and his family would be spared.

"Make an ark, a large boat," God told Noah. "I will send a flood upon the earth. It will destroy people and animals. But you and your family will be safe in the ark."

God told Noah to bring two of each kind of animal, a male and a female, into this ark. Through them, all future animals would be born.

The ark would be as big as seventy-five houses, much longer than a football field, and as tall as a three-story building. Think of the work Noah and his sons must do to make such a boat!

Noah and his family were discouraged many times as they cut trees, sawed them into beams or boards, and hammered them into place on the ark. They wanted to quit when neighbors laughed at them for building this boat far from the ocean.

But Noah obeyed God and did all that God told him to do. For a hundred and twenty years he kept on cutting, sawing, carrying, hammering and listening to his neighbors. He kept on obeying God, even when he wanted to quit.

But the day came when Noah and his family were glad that they had obeyed God. The rains fell and the waters roared up from the depths of the seas. For forty days and forty nights, the rain came down in torrents. All who were outside the ark were drowned. Inside the ark, Noah, his family and the animals were safe and dry.

GENESIS 6 & 7

1. Read 6:5-6. In these verses we read how the people had gone against God. That is what sin causes man to do. The people became _____ and God was _____ he had made them.

2. 6:7-8. What did God decide to do about this situation? _____

_____

Except, for one person....Who and Why? _____

_____

3. Read 6:9-13 Describe Noah and his family. _____

_____

(Turn back to Genesis 5:32. How old was Noah when he had sons? _____)

4. In chapter 6:14, God tells Noah to build an _____ of _____

5. How many stories will the ark be (6:16)? _____ and how many windows? _____

6. In chapter 6:19, God told Noah to bring in _____ of every kind of animal, _____ and female. In chapter 7:2-3, how many of each animal? _____ and birds? _____ Why the difference? See if you can figure this one out, and we will discuss in class.

7. Noah was to have other people in the ark besides himself. Read 6:18 and 6:10. How many people? _____ Who were they? _____

8. What happened to all the other people and animals? (Review chapter 6:7, and read chapter 7:21-23) _____

9. 7:4 tells us how long the waters came down. _____ days and _____ nights. Remember, it had never rained before!! How surprised they must have been.

10. In chapter 7, starting at verse 14, find who shut the door of the ark. _____ shut the ark, and it is found in verse _____.

11. How old was Noah when all of this took place? _____ (7:6).

FROM THIS STORY WE LEARN IT PAYS TO OBEY!

Do you suppose Noah and his family were afraid? But they obeyed didn't they, because of their trust in God. Sometimes we are afraid of the unknown, but we must trust God to take care of us just as he took such good care of Noah and his family.

Genesis 8 & 9

NOAH THANKS GOD
A Story About Promises

MEMORY VERSE: Genesis 9:13

Living on the Ark was not much fun for Noah and his family. If we tried to imagine what went on it would probably be like this....each day they fed the animals, cleaned the stalls, and did the other chores. They could not go out into the back yard or go next door to see the neighbors. There was no back yard and there were no neighbors. There was no one else in the world and nowhere else to go.

Noah and his family could not even see outside the ark. The only window was too small and too high for them to look outside.

But Noah and his family did not complain about the chores or the other problems. They were safe and dry inside the ark. Their neighbors were not, for they were drowned in the flood.

The months passed slowly on the ark. They had time to think about the things that God had done. How thankful they were that they had believed God's promise that a flood would come. How thankful they were that they had believed God when he told them to build this boat. And how thankful they were that they had believed God's promise to save Noah-and his family if they would obey him and build the Ark.

At last it was time for Noah and his family to leave the Ark. A new world smiled as they stepped outside. The sun never seemed brighter or the trees and flowers more beautiful. The animals, penned up for a year inside the Ark, romped and played upon the hills, and the birds soared high into the skies.

Noah and his family made an altar. They thanked God for saving them. They thanked God for keeping His promises.

God had another promise for Noah. "Never again will I destroy My people and animals with a flood over all the earth," He said. Then God sent a beautiful rainbow. It was a sign, a way to help Noah, and us, remember that God always keeps His promises.

GENESIS 8 and 9

1. 1 Look back in Genesis 6:5-6, why did God cause the flood to happen? List 3 reasons,

    a. _____

    b. _____

    c. _____

2. Chapter 8:1-3. God made a _____ to pass over the earth to help the waters dry up and go away. The _____ stopped. The water decreased after _____ days.

3. Genesis 8:4-6. After the Ark rested (or touched the earth) in the month, 17th day, and the water continually decreased until the _____ month, 1st day, how many months before Noah opened the window of the Ark? _____

4. First Noah send a _____ (8:7) out the window and it kept going to and fro and did not return. Then he sent out a _____ (8:8) and if you read vs. 8-12, you will know he sent the dove out _____ more times.

5. Genesis 8:16. God's instructions to Noah was to "_____ _____" of the Ark. How many people went out? _____ and what else? (vs. 17) _____

6. To give thanks to God for his safety and his family's safety, Noah did what? _____
   _____(8:20)

7. Read 8:21. Was God pleased? _____ God said he would never _____ every living thing again.

8. Genesis 9:1. God _____ Noah and his sons. What did he tell them to do? _____
   _____
   What does that mean? _____(9:19)

9. Read Genesis 9:11-14. God made a _____ with man. A sign was given as a covenant between God and man. It is a _____.

10. The covenant was not just with Noah but with his _____ (9:9).

FROM THIS STORY, YOU LEARN THAT GOD ALWAYS KEEPS HIS PROMISES. SINCE GOD KEEPS HIS PROMISES, YOU SHOULD KEEP YOURS.

What would have happened to Noah and his family if he had not obeyed God?

BIBLE HEROES

ABRAHAM

I. Remember Noah's sons: Shem, Ham and Japeth? And remember how everyone died from the flood except the ones in the ark. Now let's read Genesis 10:1. We understand that all men, nations, etc. came to be through Noah's three sons.

Shem had sons, who had sons, who had sons down to the time of Terah who had a son named Abram.

Abram took Sarai for a wife and God told them to leave the land of his father and move to Canaan. God made a promise of great blessing to Abram. He gave him this land and told him his people would become a great nation here.

Once, when there wasn't enough food in the land, Abram and Sarai went down to Egypt to get food. While they were there something unusual happened. We will discuss this from your question and answer page.

II. Abram and his brother's son Lot seemed to be very close. They were together with their families and with their possessions. Abram became a rich man and Lot also was rich. In fact, they had so many flocks and herds and tents that it was hard for them to find enough space for grazing to satisfy all their needs.

The herdsmen of both Abram and Lot began to argue and complain over the land. Abram was concerned because he didn't want any strife or family problems. He decided to divide up the land between he and Lot. Lot was given first choice and he took the land that looked the best; he took the green, lush land near the Jordan River. This did not make Abram angry, he said "Okay, I'll go the other way into the plains."

III. Abram and Sarai seemed happy except for one thing, do you know what that was? *First*, God changed their names to the names we best know them by: Abraham and to Sarah.

Then, God promised them the one thing to complete their happiness. They were doubtful at first, but trusted God in this because he had promised Abraham all along that through him a large nation would exist.

IV. In the land Lot had chosen to live were two cities, Sodom and Gomorrah. God was displeased with the terrible wickedness in these two cities and planned to destroy them.

Abraham ask God not to destroy the righteous with the wicked. He ask God to save the city if he could find 50 righteous men—God agreed. Then Abraham began to reason with God....what if there were 5 less, only 45—God agreed. Then 40, 30, 20—God agreed each time. Then Abraham asked God not to be angry with him, but what if there were only 10? Again God agreed but, alas, ten could not be found. So God planned to destroy the city. Only Lot, his wife and two daughters were saved.

Let's read Genesis 19:15, 17, 24. In verse 17 there was a special command to escape with their lives and don't look back. Someone looked back and verse 26 tells us who and what happened to that person.

V. Abraham's promise from God to father a great nation came true when his son Isaac was born to he and Sarah in their old age. Abraham was 100 and Sarah was 90. They were so happy.

God ask a hard thing of Abraham. He ask him to sacrifice his son Isaac. Abraham had faith in God; he loved God more than anyone else so he obeyed and would have sacrificed his son but God saw his great love and helped with an animal to sacrifice.

VI. Abraham's beloved wife Sarah died. He mourned her and buried her in a special place. At the age of 175 years Abraham also died and was buried in the same place as Sarah.

ABRAHAM WAS ONE OF THE MOST FAITHFUL MEN OF THE BIBLE. HIS LOVE AND TRUST IN GOD IS A GREAT EXAMPLE FOR ALL MANKIND.

BIBLE HEROES: ABRAHAM

1. Abraham's father is listed in this scripture, Gen. 11:26. _____

2. Gen. 11:28-29 gives the name of the land where Abram lived. Abram had a wife, her name is listed in Gen. 11:29. _____

3. In Gen. 12:1-4, we read about God's call to Abram. Tell about it and also about the special promise made in vs. 2-3. _____
   _____
   _____

4. Explain what Abram did in Gen. 12:10-20. _____
   _____
   _____

5. Read Gen. 13:1-5. What does it say about Abram here... also, Lot, his nephew. _____
   _____
   _____

6. Abram and Lot (his nephew) had traveled a long time together... both had much goods and animals ... strife began ... how come, and what happened? (vs. 5-12) _____
   _____
   _____

7. Abram and Sarai had their names changed. Read Gen. 17:5 and Gen. 17:15 to see their new names. _____ and _____

8. What happened in the plains of Mamre? See Gen. 18:1-15. _____
   _____
   _____

9. Abraham argued or reasoned with God, what was this about? Gen. 18:24-32 _____
   _____
   _____

10. Something special happened to Abraham when he was 100 years old, what was it? _____
    _____

11. Could you do or could your father do what Abraham did in Gen. 22:1-10? What did he do?
    _____

12. How did Abraham keep from offering his son as a sacrifice? Gen. 22:11-13? _____
_____

13. What happened to Sarah in Gen. 23:1-2 and what age was she? _____
_____

14. Read Gen. 25:7-10 and make some notations. _____
_____
_____

BIBLE HEROES: GENESIS 25-33

JACOB

For some background or history concerning Jacob's forefathers, we read in Genesis 21:2-3 how Sarah and Abraham had a son they named Isaac. Abraham proved his faith in God by agreeing to offer Isaac as a sacrifice but God stayed his hand.

Abraham's son Isaac met his wife Rebekah while watering his camels at a well. They had sons named Jacob and Esau.

GENESIS, Chapter 25

1. What was unusual about Jacob's birth? (vs. 24) _____
2. The father's name was _____ (vs. 26) and he was _____ years old. What relation was Abraham to Jacob? _____
3. What kind of men were Jacob and Esau? (vs. 27) _____
   _____
4. Jacob was his _____'s favorite son while Esau was _____'s favorite, (vs. 28)

GENESIS, Chapter 27

Father Isaac was getting older and the Bible says his eyes were dim (almost blind.)

1. Verses 1-4. Isaac asked his favorite son _____ to do something for him. What was it? _____
2. Someone did not like this. Read verses 5-10. Who overheard Isaac? _____
3. Rebekah ask her son to "_____ my voice" (vs. 8) and to bring _____ choice _____ for her to prepare (vs. 9).
4. Jacob was concerned about deceiving his father since Esau was a _____ man (vs. 11), and he was not. He was afraid he would receive a _____ rather than a _____ if he were caught (vs. 12).
5. Were they able to fool Isaac? We will read Genesis 27:18-23 and discuss in class.
6. Jacob received the blessing that went to the eldest son instead of Esau, by trickery. All of this deception caused a great rift between Jacob and Esau which lasted for many years.

GENESIS, Chapter 29

Isaac sent Jacob on a journey with some servants. They stopped to water their animals at a well in the field. While there they ask about Jacob's Uncle Laban who lived in this land. Isaac had sent Jacob to this land of his brothers to find a wife.

1. Laban had two daughters named _____ and _____. (vs. 16)

2. Jacob found he _____ Rachel and made an offer for her. It was to work _____ years for her (vs. 18).

The day of the wedding came and Laban gathered his friends in for a feast. The women wore veils and at the wedding the bride's face was covered. Jacob married a wife that night. The next morning brought a great surprise and heartache for Jacob

3. Who was Jacob's wife? (vs. 25) _____

4. When Jacob ask Uncle Laban why he had switched women, he said, "It can't be done that the younger marry before the _____." (vs. 26)

5. Verse 30. How did Jacob finally get Rachel for a wife? _____

After this Jacob left his Uncle Laban's home and returned to his home in Canaan. During his stay he had helped to make his Uncle Laban a rich man and he also became wealthy.

GENESIS, Chapter 32

1. As Jacob came home again, he was to meet his brother Esau. How did Jacob feel about this meeting? (vs. 7) _____

2. Verse 13 tells how Jacob prepared for the meeting with Esau. With _____ and verse 14 and 15 tell of some of the gifts, _____

Jacob went to much trouble preparing to meet his brother. He arranged his flocks, his wives and children and his servants in groups so that if Esau wanted to fight, some would be saved.

GENESIS, Chapter 33

1. After all of Jacob's efforts and worries, what happened when he and Esau finally met? (vs. 4) _____
2. As time went on there came a great famine to the land. Jacob, through his favorite son Joseph had moved to Egypt to live. When he died he was carried back to his home in Canaan and buried where his father and mother were buried. Do you remember where that was? Look at Genesis 50:13. The place was called _____.

JACOB HAD ANOTHER NAME .... IN PLACE OF A MEMORY VERSE, CAN YOU FIND OUT HIS OTHER NAME. _____

Abraham, Isaac and Jacob lived during the Patriarchal Age of time. They were great Patriarchs or leaders of their families. Through their teachings their families believed in God and were obedient. They were responsible for their families. Today we have the Bible to read and learn from, but our fathers too are still responsible for teaching us about God.

BIBLE HEROES: GENESIS 37-41

JOSEPH
PART I

MEMORY VERSE: Matthew 23:12

JOSEPH had 11 brothers, making 12 sons for his father Jacob. The family line was Isaac as grandfather, Jacob as father—who was the great grandfather? _____

CHAPTER 37

1. As Isaac had a favorite son... so did Jacob. Verse 3 tells us who it was _____ and Verse 4 tells us how the other brothers felt about this _____

2. One way Jacob showed his favoritism to Joseph was by a special gift. What was that? (vs. 3) _____

3. Joseph was a dreamer. Verses 5-7 tell us about one of his dreams. What was it? _____
   _____

   In class we will discuss further how these dreams got Joseph in trouble with his family. (vs. 5-11)

4. Jacob sent Joseph to check on his brothers who were watching over the flocks at some grazing land away from home. When the brothers saw him coming they said, "Look, this _____ is coming." (vs. 19) What plans did they have for Joseph? (vs. 18-20)
   _____

5. One brother did not want to go along with the plan. Verse 22 tells us his name. _____

6. Read verses 23-27... so what did happen to Joseph? _____
   _____
   _____

7. Now Rueben was away when the other brothers put their plan into action. Verse 29 and 22 tell us what Rueben had previously planned to do. What was that? _____
   _____

8. How did the brothers break the news to their father of Joseph's disappearance? (vs. 31-33)
   _____
   _____

9. Did Jacob take this news very well? _____ Verse 35 tells us his reaction. _____
   _____

28

10.   Meantime, where was Joseph? (vs. 36) _____

CHAPTER 39

11.   Joseph was not forgotten in this far off land. (Vs. 2) _____ was with him.

12.   His master _____ (vs. 1) was an _____ in Pharaoh's army.

13.   Was Potiphar pleased with Joseph's services? _____ (vs. 4-6)

14.   BUT there was something dark brewing. Potiphar had a wife who had her eye on Joseph. She tried every way possible to get Joseph to pay special attention to her and he would not. Alter all, she was his master's wife. Since she could not persuade him, she tried to trick him by grabbing hold of his coat. In Verse 12 it states he left his garment behind and _____ outside.

15.   Verse 16 tells us she kept his garment and showed Potiphar when he _____.

16.   Her lies caused Potiphar to become angry and he put Joseph in _____. (vs. 20)

17.   Even in prison Joseph's trustworthiness showed. He had favor in the sight of the prison keeper and was put in charge of _____ prisoners, (vs. 21,22)

CHAPTER 40

18.   Joseph made friends and was liked by the prisoners. One day Pharaoh recalled his former butler and baker and Joseph ask a favor of the butler. Verse 14 tells us what the favor was _____ and verse 23 tells us if the butler did what was asked, _____

CHAPTER 41

19.   Poor Joseph... .how did he finally get out of prison? (vs. 9,12) _____
_____

20.   How long was Joseph in prison? (vs. 1) _____

In chapter 41 there are two dreams that Pharaoh had and no one could interpret them. After the butler remembered what he knew of Joseph in prison ... he had told him what his dream meant.... he told Pharaoh about Joseph. In class we will read about these two dreams and discuss Joseph's interpretation of them in class. If you want to read them ahead of time, they are in Verses 17-21 and verses 22-24. Also, find the verse in Chapter 41 that tells you Joseph did not take credit for interpretation. _____

FROM THIS STORY WE LEARN
THAT JEALOUSY CAUSES PEOPLE
TO DO TERRIBLE THINGS.

BIBLE HEROES: GENESIS 41-50

JOSEPH
PART II

MEMORY VERSE: Genesis 46:3

As part of the dream interpretation of the famine to come, Joseph told Pharaoh God said to do certain things. Read verses 33-34; we'll discuss in class.

CHAPTER 41

1. In verse 39, 40, Pharaoh appointed _____ to oversee the preparation for the bad years.

2. How old was Joseph when he assumed this important job? (vs. 46) _____

3. During the 7 years of plenty, Joseph had two sons named _____ (vs. 51) and _____ (vs. 52).

4. Verses 47 & 48 tells us what Joseph did during the 7 plenteous years. What? _____
_____

5. Then what happened? (vs. 53) _____
_____

6. All Egypt and surrounding countries had a famine. What did they do to survive? (vs. 56-57)
_____

CHAPTER 42

7. Back in the land where Jacob and Joseph's brothers lived, there were hard times. Jacob gave instructions to his sons. (See vs. 2) _____
_____

8. Jacob sent his sons to Egypt to buy corn. All of his sons but one. _____ did not go. (vs. 4)

9. The brothers came before Joseph to buy grain. What was strange about their meeting? (vs. 8) _____

10. Joseph accused his brothers of being _____. (vs. 9)

11. To assure Joseph that they are not spies, they explain their situation. Verse 13 tells it _____
_____

12. In verse 22, Reuben reminds the brothers of something in their past. What was it? _____
_____

13. In verses 23 & 24, we read of some feelings Joseph had towards his brothers. _____
_____

14. What did Joseph tell them to do to prove they were telling the truth? (vs. 20) _____
_____

Joseph had one of the brothers, Simon stay behind when they returned to their home. They were to bring their youngest brother Benjamin with them when they returned. After some time passed, they were getting low on food again and it was time to go back to Egypt and get grain from this man they had met before. Remember, they still did not know it was their brother Joseph.

CHAPTER 43

15. Jacob (the father) reluctantly agreed to let Benjamin go down with them to Egypt. Judah made him a promise, (vs. 8-9) What was it? _____
_____

16. Joseph was overcome by his feelings for his family and went to his (vs. 30) _____ and _____. Then (vs. 31) _____ his face and went out again to eat with them.

17. Read verse 26. Does it remind you of something in Joseph's earlier life? As a reminder, read Chpt. 37:5-7. Tell about it. _____

CHAPTER 45

18. After a while Joseph made himself known to his brothers. Read verses 1-5. What did he say to them? (vs. 4) _____

19. In verse 5, Joseph told his brothers not to worry about what had happened because it was part of _____'s plan.

20. What did Jacob (Israel) say when his sons told him about Joseph? (vs. 28) _____
_____

CHAPTER 46

21. What instructions did God give to Jacob (Israel)? (vs. 2-3) _____
_____

22. Pharaoh told Joseph to bring his family to Egypt because of the famine. All the family came to Egypt bringing their flocks and belongings. Verse 29 tells us that father (Jacob) and son (Joseph) finally met again at _____.

CHAPTER 50

23. When Jacob died, Joseph took his body back to their land and buried him with his ancestors in the Cave of _____ (vs. 13)

24. Joseph died in Egypt at age _____. (vs. 26) Before he died he told his brothers God would be directing them to return to their homeland in Canaan. He ask that they do something for him when they returned home. What was it? (vs. 24-25) _____
_____

BIBLE HEROES: Exodus, Chapter 1-3

MOSES
Part I

MEMORY VERSE: Exodus 3:14

BACKGROUND:

Joseph's family moved to Egypt during the time of the great famine. After Joseph and his brothers had grown old and died, their families (the Israelites) grew in numbers to a great nation.

Meanwhile, a new Pharaoh ruled the land. He felt no obligation to Joseph's people. In fact, he and his people made slaves of them, requiring them to work hard under cruel masters. BUT, the more the Egyptians mistreated them, the more their families grew until their number was alarming to the Egyptians.

MOSES BIRTH—Exodus 1 & 2

1. (1:15-16) How did Pharaoh try to control the growth of the Israelites? _____

2. (1:17) Was Pharaoh's plan successful? _____ Why? _____

3. (2:1-2) How did Moses' family save him? _____

MOSES GROWS UP—Exodus 2

1. What did Moses do to try to right a wrong to his fellow Israelite? (Vs.11-12) _____

2. It backfired !!!—What happened? (Vs. 13 & 14) _____

3. What did Moses do? (Vs. 15) _____

4. (Read Exodus 2:21-22). Moses wife was _____ His son's name was _____.

5. Read verse 24. What covenant does this verse refer to? (Remember back, or refer back to your first sheets on Abraham.) _____

GOD HAS A MISSION FOR MOSES—Exodus 3

1. How did God get Moses attention? (Vs. 1 & 2) _____
   _____

2. What had God observed about the condition of His people, the Israelites? (Vs. 7) _____
   _____

3. What task did God give Moses? (Vs. 10) _____
   _____

4. Who was Moses to say sent him to be their leader? (Vs. 14) _____

5. Who was Moses to go and speak to? (Vs. 16) _____

6. What was the message he was to deliver? (Vs. 17) _____
   _____

EXODUS 5-11

MOSES
Part II

A Story About Power

For many years pharaoh had kept Moses' people, the Hebrews, in slavery. He had made them work hard, building cities for him. Of course pharaoh did not pay them. He gave them only enough food to keep them strong for his work, and a tiny hut to live in.

GOD DID NOT WANT HIS PEOPLE TO BE SLAVES.

God spoke to Moses in a special way and sent him hack to Egypt. God wanted Moses to tell pharaoh to let the people go. And God chose Moses' brother Aaron to help him.

"God says you must let my people go free," Moses told pharaoh. But pharaoh was angry. He would not give up all that free work.

To show God's power, Aaron threw down his shepherd's rod and it became a snake. Surely no one else could do that. But pharaoh's magicians had some strange power. When they threw down their rods, they became snakes too. You can imagine how surprised Moses and Aaron were to see that! But God showed He was more powerful than the Egyptian gods. Aaron's snake ate up all the other snakes!

On the next visit, Moses and Aaron caused the first of the ten plagues to come to the land of Egypt. Each one of them became more terrible than the one before.

The first was the plague of blood, when Moses touched the Nile River and the water turned to blood.

Moses and Aaron came back to pharaoh to bring another plague. This time they caused frogs to come up on the land by the thousands.

The next time Moses and Aaron came to pharaoh, they caused a plague of lice and gnats to go on all the animals of Egypt. God's power was showing; but pharaoh's heart was hard and he wouldn't listen to them.

Swarms of flies came next. This time Moses told pharaoh that God would divide the people and the flies would only come upon the Egyptians. God would not let them come to His people. After God sent the flies, pharaoh said the people should worship their God but they could not go free.

The next plague God sent caused the cattle, the horses and many other animals to become sick and die. Now pharaoh and his people began to be afraid of God's wondrous power.

Another plague made painful boils break out upon all the Egyptian people and on the animals that were left. Many of the Egyptian people began to believe that the God of Moses was the most powerful. But pharaoh's heart just got harder and he would not admit it. He still would not let the people go.

When hail came and destroyed most of the crops of Egypt, that showed that God was greater than all the Egyptian gods of the harvest. Now pharaoh sent for Moses and Aaron. He said he was wrong and if they would stop the hail he would let the people go. But he didn't stick to his word...he wouldn't let them go.

One day darkness came across the land. It was so thick they could feel it and their lamps wouldn't make any light. But it came only to the Egyptians. God's people, the children of Israel, had light in their homes.

Then a plague worse than darkness came. All the firstborn animals and people died, even pharaoh's oldest son. It was clear now that God controlled life and death. Now pharaoh and his people feared Moses' God, for they thought much about life and death, and feared for their lives.

At last the contest was over. Moses' God was more powerful than all the gods of Egypt. The magicians, the Egyptian people, and even pharaoh, all knew that now.

****

The Ten Plagues

MEMORY VERSE: After you have completed the exercise on the next page, learn what the ten plagues were and recite them for your memory verse points—

I know every one of you can do that—easily!!!

1. Who did God give Moses for a helper in going before Pharaoh to help the Israelites? _____ (7:1)
2. What happened to Aaron's rod? _____(7:9.10)
3. How many plagues were there? Name them below and put a check in the column that applies to that plague.

PLAGUES	Exodus	Hardened Pharaoh's Heart	Would Let Them Go	Changed His Mind
	7:19, 22			
	8:5, 8, 15			
	8:16, 19			
	8:24, 28, 32			
	9:3, 7			
	9:9, 12			
	9:23, 28, 34-35			
	10:12, 20			
	10:21, 27			
	11:5, 12:31			

4. Every time a new plague was to begin, God told Moses to hold out what? (Exodus 7:19; 8:5, 17) _____
5. How did the Israelites protect their families in the last plague? Exodus 12:3,7 _____
   _____
   _____
6. Who won the contest between God and Pharaoh? _____

FACT: God is more powerful than anyone else . Moses was able to do these mighty works because God was using him to accomplish His plan for his people (the Israelites).

EXODUS

MOSES
Part III: Crossing the Red Sea

A Story of Trust

"What have we done?" Pharaoh began to wonder. "We have let all those slaves go free and have lost their work."

Pharaoh had begun to see how much work the Hebrews had done. Now that they were gone, who was there to do this work? He began to see how much work would not get done without them.

Pharaoh ordered men to get his chariot and prepare his army for battle. He had heard how the Hebrews were moving about in the wilderness and thought they must surely not know where they were going. His spies must have told him how the Israelites were trapped at a camp by the sea and how easy it would be to conquer them there.

So Pharaoh's chariots, horsemen, and troops pursued as quickly as they could and found the Israelites trapped by the sea. Moses knew why they were there, of course, for the Lord had told him. But the people of Israel did not know. They were terrified to see Pharaoh and his chariots and horsemen approaching. They were sure that they could not escape for they didnot trust the Lord to save them. Some began to complain to Moses.

"Why have you brought us out here to die?" they said. "Didn't we tell you to leave us in Egypt? It would be better to serve the Egyptians there than die out here." "Don't be afraid," said Moses. "Trust the Lord and see how He will deliver you. The Lord will fight for you."

As evening came, the Lord moved the cloud that led the Israelites until it was between them and the Egyptians. The Egyptian army had to stop, for they could not see where they were going.

At the Lord's command, Moses stretched out his rod and his hand across the sea. All night the Lord drove the sea apart with a strong wind and made a path across the sea on dry land. When morning came, Moses led his people to the other side of the sea, with a wall of water on each side of them. Moses and his people trusted God to keep the water there until they had crossed.

At the right moment, the Lord took His cloud away, and the Egyptian army pursued. But when they reached the sea, the Lord let the waters rush back upon them and they were drowned.

Now the people of Israel saw how the Lord could do great miracles to save His people. They knew that they had not trusted Him fully. It was an important lesson for them to learn, one they would have to learn again and again in the wilderness.

EXODUS Chapter 6
1. As Moses led the people out of Egypt, where were they going? (vs. 8) _____
_____

Chapter 14
2. As the children of Israel left Egypt, Pharaoh had second thoughts. Verse 8 tells us what he did. _____
_____

3. The people were afraid. In verse 13, Moses told them to do certain things. What were they?
_____

4. Verse 21 says Moses stretched out his hand over the sea and it parted; verse 16 tells us the object that was important in this action. _____

5. Read verses 26 and 28. What happened to the Egyptians? _____
_____

Chapter 16
6. Through Moses request of God food was provided, (vs.11-15) _____
and _____.

7. How long did the people eat this kind of food? (vs. 35) _____
This was how long they wandered in the wilderness.

Chapter 17
8. Another time Moses provided water for the people. How did God tell him to get this water? (vs. 3-6) _____

Chapter 16
9. Did the people ever go hungry? _____ What was the quantity of food provided? (vs. 21)
_____

Chapter 18
10. Moses also helped the people in other ways. (vs. 13 and 16) Read these verses and we will discuss this in class.

Chapter 19
11. Moses led the people to an area called Sinai where some great things happened. The area was desert and also _____ (vs. 2).

Next week we will discuss things that happened to the Israelites here at Sinai and also the great things Moses did. Remember all of these miracles and all of the protection for this great nation of people was done because of God's love and care for them. He had made a promise to Abraham many years ago that this nation of people would be a large nation and they would live in a special place He had' planned for them.

FROM THIS LESSON WE CAN LEARN THAT
IF WE TRUST IN GOD, HE WILL TAKE CARE OF US.

MOSES
Part IV: Leading the People and Receiving God's Law

MEMORY VERSE: Exodus 19:5

THIS IS A STORY ABOUT SOME SPECIAL PEOPLE. THEY WERE GOD'S SPECIAL PEOPLE, THE ISRAELITES.

This is a story, a true story from the Bible, and i want you to fill in the blanks as much as you can.

The Israelite people were in Egypt because there was a (flood, famine) in the land where they lived. They had come here because of a relative, a (brother, son) had been there for a long time and his name was (Simon, Joseph). He was in Egypt because his (father, brothers) hated him and sold him to some traders.

After a time, these people became so large a group that the Egyptians were afraid they would try to take over their land and so they made them (kings, slaves). God did not like his people to be slaves so he sent a man to help them get away. The Pharaoh refused to let them go until God sent a plague where the (first born, middle child) was killed in every household. This was the tenth plague. There had been plagues of (water turning to blood, water turning into wine). So Pharaoh let the people go to the land God had promised them, a land flowing with (tea, milk) and (jelly, honey).

To get to this land they must travel far and the Egyptians had decided to follow them and try to get them back. As they were traveling they came to the (Purple Sea, Red Sea) where God stopped the water to let them cross over. The water (stood high, got them wet) as they crossed over and then the Egyptians started into the sea to cross too, but the (fish, water) ran back and they were all (sleepy, drowned).

The people complained about the food and water. So God sent them (quail, pigeons) for meat and (crackers, manna) for bread and so they traveled on toward this promised land.

Today's lesson takes up their journey and we will begin on the next page. These people live through some exciting times and some hard times, but their leader (John the Baptist, Moses) with the help of his brother Aaron kept them going.

Background:

God used Moses to lead the Hebrew people out of Egypt. God protected them from the Egyptians, provided them with water and meat and bread, and gave them Moses and Aaron to lead them through the wilderness.

They had traveled for 3 months and were at a special place called Sinai in front of a mountain. At Sinai God restated his promise to make a great nation of the people who descended from Abraham, Isaac, and Jacob.

God told Moses to prepare the people to hear Him and receive his word. The people said that they were eager to do as God said, but as we so often see, they were impatient and gave in to selfish material concerns.

Exodus, Chapter 19

1. vs. 1 Where were the people? _____
2. vs. 5-6 God said that if the people would _____ him they would be His own people, a _____ treasure, and a _____ nation.
3. vs. 8 How did the people answer? _____
4. vs. 10, 12 What 2 instructions did God give the people?
    a. _____
    b. _____
5. vs. 17-18 Where were the people? _____
   How did God appear? _____
6. vs 19 What sounds were made? _____

The Lord called Moses to the top of the Mountain. He told Moses to go back and remind the people not to touch the mountain and then to come back up.

Chapter 20

7. Moses did as God instructed and when he returned to the mountain God gave Moses special laws. What is Exodus 20 about? _____

8. Summarize the commandments in the following verses:
   3 _____
   4 _____
   7 _____
   8 _____
   12 _____

13 _____

14 _____

15 _____

16 _____

17 _____

Chapters 21-31
Skip this section. We will complete this in class.

9. In addition to what we call the Ten Commandments, God gave Moses many other rules to live by. Use the headings in these chapters to list 8 more things God gave instructions about.

   1. _____ 5. _____

   2. _____ 6. _____

   3. _____ 7. _____

   4. _____ 8. _____

10. Ch. 25:10-22 gives instructions for building something. What was it? _____

    Vs. 16 What would be kept in it? _____

11. Some of God's instructions were written down. What were they written on? Ch 31:18

    _____

    How were they written? _____

Chapter 32

12. All these instructions from God took some time, and the people waiting for Moses' return became impatient. Read verses 1-4 and tell what they did? _____

13. Vs. 9-10 God saw what the people did. Was he angry? _____ What did he plan to do to them? _____

14. Moses pleaded with God. What happened in verse 14? _____

15. Vs. 19-20 When Moses came down from the Mountain what did he see? _____

    What happened to the tablets? _____

What happened to the calf? _____

16. Vs. 34 God told Moses to take the people on to the promised land, but that one day they would be punished for their _____.

17. In Exodus 32:9, 33:3, 33:5, God said the Israelites were _____.
What does this mean? _____
Do you agree that they were like that? _____ Give an example _____
_____

Chapter 34

18. Vs 1 God told Moses to prepare two _____. Why: _____

19. Where did Moses go? vs. 2 _____
Vs. 28 How long was he there? _____
What was written? _____

20. Vs. 29-30 When Moses came down this time, something was unusual about him. What was it? _____

21. The people were afraid and amazed, but this showed them God's power and glory. In spite of their weakness and unfaithfulness God took care of these people and used them to accomplish his plans for all people. Remember, He had made promises to _____, _____, and _____. (32:13, 33:1)
What was the promise? _____

Moses' journey with the Israelites began in Genesis and has continued through the book of Exodus. They continue on their trip through the books of Leviticus, Numbers, and Deuteronomy. We will learn more about how they finally finish the journey in our next lessons.

The books of Genesis, Exodus, Leviticus, Numbers, and Deuteronomy contain many laws which God gave man to live by. Sometimes these five books are called the books of Law. They are also referred to as the Pentateuch. BONUS Use a dictionary to find out what Pentateuch means.

44

GOD GAVE THE TEN COMMANDMENTS FOR THE ISRAELITES TO LIVE BY ....
DO WE LIVE BY SIMILAR COMMANDMENTS TODAY?

I. Thou shalt have no other gods before me. Exodus 20:1

Mark 12:29-30 _____

II. Thou shalt not make unto thee any graven images. Exodus 20:4

1 Cor. 10:14; 1 John 5:21 _____

III. Thou shalt not take the name of the Lord thy God in vain. Exodus 20:7

Matt. 5:34-37 _____

IV. Remember the Sabbath day to keep it holy. Exodus 20:8

Acts 20:7 _____

V. Honor thy father and thy mother that you may live long upon the land. Exodus 20:12

Eph. 6:2-3 _____

VI. Thou shalt not kill. Exodus 20:13

Matt. 5:21-22 _____

VII. Thou shalt not commit adultery. Exodus 20:4

Matt. 5:27-28 _____

VIII. Thou shalt not steal. Exodus 20:15

Matt. 19:18; Rom 13:9 _____

IX. Thou shalt not bear false witness against thy neighbor. Exodus 20:16

Matt. 19:18: Rom. 13:9 _____

X. Thou shalt not covet thy neighbor's house, wife, servant or animals. Exodus 20:17

Rom. 7:7; 13:9 _____

In the margin of your sheet, put a yes or no if we do or do not keep this commandment today.

God gave these and other laws to the Israelites at Mt. Sinai. This was a period called the Mosaic time. We now live in the Christian time, but as we can see from the New Testament, some of these same laws are for us today... but not every one of them. We need to be careful and be sure we are living under the New Testament rules that Jesus taught when He was here on earth and that God has guided special men to write down for us.

Exodus and Leviticus

MORE LAW

MEMORY VERSE: Ex. 40: 38 or Ex. 28:1

In addition to the Ten Commandments, God gave Moses laws for living by and laws for worshipping Him. He established a tribe of priests to conduct ceremonies, make sacrifices, and accept offerings from the people. The priests were called Levites because they were descendants of Levi, the son of Jacob. (**Do you remember the other sons of Jacob?) Ex.1:1-4

The last half of Exodus and the book of Leviticus contain thousands of rules. The rules were interpreted and enforced by the Levites, who used the laws to help the people make atonement to God for their sins. There were so many laws that it was impossible to keep all of them, but God used the laws to teach us that He expects us to obey Him in every part of our lives. Under the laws of the Old Testament, sins were not forgiven and there was no baptism for the remission of sins.

The only thing people could do about their sins was to go to the priest and make sacrifices as he told them to. The sacrifices would serve as a means of atonement, that is, it would just "cover" their sins or "roll them forward" until their next appointed sacrifice, ceremony, or feast.

Remember, the Israelites were on the move, wandering through the desert, so they needed a portable place to worship. The books of Exodus and Leviticus also give very detailed instructions for making a Tabernacle (a portable Temple), altars, an ark for carrying the stone tablets, and for setting up the Tabernacle and the surrounding area.

1. Ex 2:1 Moses' parents were both descendants of _____.

2. Ex 4:14 Moses' brother was _____ the _____.

3. Ex 28:1 _____ and his sons were chosen to minister to God as _____.

4. Identify these objects which were used in worship. Ex 35, verse:

    11 _____ - The tent for worship

    12 _____ - The chest which held the tablets

    13 _____ - for the shewbread

    14 _____ - for light

15 _____ altar

16 altar of _____

17 _____ of the court

18 _____ of the tabernacle

19 _____ of the ministry for _____ and his sons.

All of these items were carefully handcrafted according to the instructions God gave. Collections were made from the people for the materials. They gave gold, silver, bronze, fine linen and yarn, special woods, oils, onyx and other stones like emeralds, sapphires, diamonds and amethysts!

The priests were responsible for overseeing the construction of these items, and also for moving them from place to place, and erecting the tabernacle when they reached their new campsite.

Ex 40:36-38 and Numbers 9:16-22 tell us how the tabernacle was related to their wandering. .

What was over the tabernacle in the day? _____

What was over the tabernacle in the night? _____

How did the people know when to move? _____

BONUS: Look up the word <u>atonement</u> in a dictionary,

atonement - _____

_____

Is there anything in New Testament Christianity which compares to atonement. How would New Testament Christians atone for their sins?

NUMBERS and DEUTERONOMY

WEAKNESS IN THE WILDERNESS

MEMORY VERSE: Numbers 14:8

In the book of Numbers all of the people were accounted for by a census. Each family was listed with its tribe, from the 12 sons of Jacob. (Each son represented a tribe.) It is also a book of continued wandering in the wilderness.

In Numbers and Deuteronomy we will see lapses in faith, weakness, wanderings, the deaths of Moses and Aaron, and the emergence of a new leader.

1. Numbers 1:1 At this point, how long have the people been out of Egypt? _____
   _____

2. Numbers 11:1 What did the people do that displeased God? _____
   Will they NEVER change?

3. It is now less than three years they have been in the wilderness and they are on the edge of the promised land. The land has been promised to them and they have God to help them, but let's see what they do.

4. Num. 13:1-2 Moses sent men to do what? _____
   vs 4-15 How many were sent? _____
   vs 27-28, 32-33 How did the majority of the spies report? _____

5. Because of this report the Israelites were scared & refused to go into the promised land, but two spies were NOT afraid. Who were they? Num. 14:6 _____

6. vs 7-9 They said, the land is exceedingly _____. The Lord will bring us into
   the land and _____. Joshua and Caleb said, "... the Lord is _____
   us. Do not _____ them."

But the people WERE afraid and refused to enter. The Lord was very disappointed in the people because of their lack of faith and He even thought about killing them all.

7. vs 27-34 God said that the carcasses of those who murmured would _____ in
   the wilderness. This means they would die there. Only _____ and
   _____ would live long enough to enter the land. So, because of their lack
   _____ of faith, the Israelites were caused to wander for _____ years.

They were SO close and could have ended their journey by just trusting in God to do what He had promised that He would do. But their fears and weaknesses caused them to wander about and die in the wilderness. Only the faithful, Joshua and Caleb, and the young people were ever allowed into the promised land.

Moses continued to struggle with the Israelites in the wilderness. The people's murmuring and rebellion must have been frustrating to Moses, Aaron and Joshua and Caleb as well. Their continual complaining may have led to Moses' mistake in judgement.

Numbers 20 tells about his mistake.

8. vs 2 What was their problem? _____

9. vs 6 What did Moses and Aaron do? _____

10. vs 7-8 Did God have an answer to their problem? _____

    a. What did God tell Moses and Aaron to take with them? _____

    b. What did He tell them to do to the rock? _____

11. vs 9-11 How did Moses get water from the rock? _____

12. vs 12 Moses had to pay for his mistake. God said, "Because you did not believe me… you shall NOT _____

13. vs 13 Where did this happen? _____

14. vs 24-29 Did Aaron make it to the promised land? _____ Why? _____
    _____

15. If Moses would not be allowed to lead the people into the promised land, and Aaron was dead, WHO do you think might make a good leader? _____ Look back through today's lesson

Numbers 27

16. vs 12-13 Did Moses ever SEE the promised land? _____

17. vs 15-20 After seeing the land, Moses talked to the Lord and the Lord told him to <u>inaugurate</u> a new leader. Who was the man? _____ Did he take over ALL authority from Moses right away? _____

In the book of Deuteronomy we see Moses and Joshua leading the people for many more years, but, as God predicted, Moses finally died in the wilderness.

18. Look to the <u>last few chapters</u> of <u>Deuteronomy</u> and find:

    a. (33:1) Moses made his final _____

50

b. (34:5) Moses dies at _____

c. (34:7) How old was he? _____

19. Copy verses 9 and 10: _____

_____

_____

_____

12 Books Of History

Joshua	*II Samuel*	*II Chronicles*
Judges	*I Kings*	*Ezra*
Ruth	*II Kings*	*Nehemiah*
1 Samuel	*I Chronicles*	*Esther*

JOSHUA

RAHAB

A Story About Kindness

MEMORY VERSE: Joshua 1:3 or Joshua 1:5

"Go into The Promised Land and find out what you can," Joshua told two spies. "Look especially at Jericho."

The people of Israel were ready to go into The Promised Land to live. But they must first fight the people who lived there and conquer them. If they didn't, they would be driven back into the wilderness or would all be killed.

The two spies crossed the Jordan River and went to Jericho. That was the first city the Israelites must conquer. The spies must learn whatever they could to help their people win in a battle.

The spies stayed at a house built on Jericho's wall. The owner, a woman named Rahab, rented rooms to travelers. But someone saw the men come into Jericho and told the king. The king sent men to capture them.

When Rahab heard that the king's men were coming, she hid the spies under some flax on her rooftop. Then she told the king's men, "They were here, but they left just before sunset in time to get outside the city gate. Hurry, and you may catch them."

As soon as the King's men left, Rahab went up to the rooftop to have a talk with the spies. "I know that the Lord has already given this land to you," she said. "Our people are afraid of you because of the miracles which the Lord has done for you. I have shown kindness to you by keeping you safe, so please show kindness to me and my family when you conquer Jericho."

"You have been kind and saved our lives, so we will be kind and save yours," the spies said. "But you must tie this scarlet cord in your window. When we come to conquer, whoever is in the house will be saved. Whoever is outside the house will be killed." Rahab agreed, and tied the scarlet cord in her window. It would remind the men and their army of Rahab's kindness, and of their promise to be kind to her.

Chapter 2

1. Before crossing over the Jordan River, Joshua the new leader of God's people sent _____ men to _____ out the land. (vs. 1)

2. The king of Jericho heard that two Israelites had entered the city. He sent men to a house belonging to _____ (vs. 3) to check this out.

3. How did Rahab protect the two men? Two things she did (vs, 4) _____

   (vs. 5) _____

4. How did she hide them? (vs. 6) _____

5. Rahab explained to the two men how the people of her land feared God and knew how he had protected them. She told of the miracle God had done to free them from the Egyptians. What was it? (vs. 10) _____

6. Since Rahab had protected them, she ask for something in return for her family. What was it? _____

7. The men said if she would not give them away, they would deal kindly with her family. Their statement was "Our _____." (vs. 14)

8. Where was Rahab's house located? _____ (vs. 15)

9. How did they escape? _____ (vs. 15)

10. How long were they to hide in the mountains? _____ (vs. 16)

11. There was to be a sign between them so Rahab's family would be protected. What was it? _____ (vs. 18)

12. Another restriction was put on Rahab and her family. Tell about it. (vs. 18, 19) _____

13. What would void the agreement between the two Israelites and Rahab? (vs 20) _____

Chapter 6

14. (Vs. 23-2) What happened to Rahab when Joshua and the Israelites took the city? _____

WE LEARN FROM THIS STORY HOW ONE KINDNESS DESERVES OR ENCOURAGES ANOTHER KINDNESS.

TAKE THE ATTACHED RED (SCARLET) STRING AND HANG IT SOMEWHERE IN YOUR ROOM TO REMIND YOU TO BE KIND TO OTHERS; ESPECIALLY YOUR FAMILY.

BIBLE HEROES

JOSHUA

Crossing the Jordan to Jericho

Where is your memory verse? _____

When Joshua's spies (the ones that Rahab had helped) returned to camp, they reported that the inhabitants there were afraid of the Israelites because they had heard of the miracles God had performed on their behalf. They believed that surely God would deliver the land to them.

So, Joshua prepared the people to cross over the Jordan River and on the day they were to cross over, the Lord spoke to Joshua.

Chapter 3

1. In verse 7 the Lord said to Joshua, "This day I will begin to _____ you in the sight of all Israel, that they may know that, as I. was with _____, so I will be with you."

2. Verses 14-17 tell how they got across the river.
   As they approached the river, who walked in front? _____
   Who entered the water first? _____
   What happened to the water? _____
   How long did the water stay that way? _____

Chapter 4

3. In verses 4-9 Joshua set up a memorial to mark the place where Israel crossed over the Jordan into the promised land.
   How many men were asked to help? _____
   What did they use to mark the spot? _____
   Why 12? _____

Chapter 5

4. Verse 6 tells how long it took them to get there and why* Do you remember this? Summarize this verse.

5. In verses 10-12 it tells where they were camped and what they were eating. What was the place? _____
   What did they start eating? _____

What did they stop eating? _____

Chapter 6

6. The city of Jericho was securely _____, no-one was going _____ or _____ (vs.1). Why do you think it was this way? _____
_____

7. In verses 2-5 God gives them instructions on how to take Jericho.

   He told them to march around the city _____ time for _____ days,

   And as they marched, seven _____ should carry seven _____

   in front of the _____,

   Then on the _____ day they should march around the city _____ times

   And on their last trip around the city the priests should _____

   and the people should _____.

8. We will read verses 15, 16, and 20 in class to see how it happened.

9. In verse 21 it says they utterly destroyed _____ that was in the city, both _____ and _____, young and old, ox and sheep and donkey. Did they really destroy ALL who were there, or was there an exception? Read the rest of the chapter to find out.

10. Verse 27 is your memory verse. Copy it down three times. _____
_____
_____
_____
_____
_____
_____
_____
_____

LIVING IN THE PROMISED LAND

MEMORY VERSE: Josh 23:11 or 24:15

Taking the Land

So, the Israelites finally made it into the Promised Land under the leadership of Joshua. The first city they overtook was Jericho. We have studied about how they did that. What do you think made the walls of Jericho fall... the marching? the trumpets? or maybe the shouting? Read Joshua 6:16 for the answer. _____

God continued to help them take the land, sometimes using great miracles in order to keep the promise He had made to Abraham, Isaac and Jacob.

Remember, God had promised them as much land as they could _____ over. Gen.13:17

In addition to Jericho, we read about many other places that they took. Skim over these verses and list some of the places they spread through:

1. Josh 8:1 What town and King? _____
2. Josh 10:1 What town made peace with the Israelites? _____
3. Josh 10:11-13 God helped Joshua defend Gibeon with two miracles. List them _____
   _____
4. Josh 11:16 List 6 regions God gave them:

   _____   _____

   _____   _____

   _____   _____

5. Josh 12:9-24 About how many kingdoms did they conquer? _____
6. When they had been given all the land that the sole of their foot had trod upon, they divided up the land among the twelve tribes. Look at Josh. 15:20-62. About how many cities did the tribe of Judah take? _____

The Promise Fulfilled

7. We will read Josh 21:43-45 in class. Summarize its content here: _____
   _____

Joshua's Farewell

8. In chapters 23 and 24 Joshua retells the story of how they got out of Egypt, traveled through

the wilderness, and received the land God had promised.

In 23:8 he reminds them to _____ the Lord.

In 23:11 he tells them they should _____ the Lord.

In 24:14 &23 he warns them to _____ other gods.

9. Joshua 24:15 is a very famous Bible verse. It is quite long, but worth memorizing. Copy the entire verse here, try to remember as much of it as you can, then, in class I will show you a short version that a lot of people memorize. _____

_____

_____

_____

_____

10. What happens in verse 29? _____

11. Years before, someone had made a special request. Read verse 32 and see if you remember the person and the request. _____

12. We have now covered the Pentateuch which means _____ and the book of Joshua. In the first five books, God dealt with man directly and through "fatherly" leaders like A_____, I_____, and J_____; then he led the people through wise men like M_____ and J_____ who helped them into this promised land which is also called Canaan.

13. In our future studies, God will set up <u>Judges</u> and then <u>Kings</u> to govern the people. What book follows Joshua in the Old Testament? _____

Our next lesson will be from that book.

MIX AND MATCH

ESTHER   JOB   MOSES   DAVID   NOAH   ABRAHAM   ADAM

Directions: Match the names in the list below with the names listed above.

Aaron	Mordecai	Eliphaz	Bathsheba	Abel	Seth	Sarah
Animals	Joseph	Lot	Esau	Haman	Jonathan	Uriah
Bildad	Cain	Isaac	Miriam	Jacob	Serpent	God
Solomon	Zophar	Joshua	King Saul	Eve	Rebekah	

JUDGES

The Book and the Servants

MEMORY VERSE: Judges 13:24

_____
_____
_____

The Israelites now occupied Canaan, the Promised Land. While they had defeated many armies and taken several cities, they still had many enemies to overcome. They needed military leadership as well as spiritual leaders because some of them were being influenced by pagan tribes who worshipped other gods or idols.

Their own leaders—Moses, Aaron, & Joshua had all died and the people were confused about who should lead them.

Many times, as the children of Israel encountered problems, they asked God for a leader and He provided one.

1. Read Judges 3:9, 3:15, 4:3, and 6:7. What words do they have in common? _____
_____

2. Use these verses to identify the various JUDGES who served God by helping His people:

   Judges 3:9 _____
   3:15 _____
   3:31 _____
   4:4 _____
   4:8 _____ (ruled with Deborah)
   6:22 _____
   9:22 _____
   10:1-2 _____
   10:3 _____
   12:7 _____
   12:8 _____
   12:11 _____
   12:13 _____
   and finally 13:24 _____

Some of the judges were great military leaders, but others helped the people return to God after they had done evil. Samson is probably the judge you have heard of the most. He was a special child who was given by God to a man Manoah and his wife who dedicated Samson's life to the Lord. An angel told them that he was to be raised as a Nazarite. He was a judge and a special servant to God.

BIBLE HEROES

GIDEON
A STORY ABOUT COURAGE

MEMORY VERSE: Judges 6:16

"You have too many soldiers," the Lord told Gideon. Gideon was surprised. How can an army have too many soldiers, especially when it is going to fight a much larger army?

Gideon was going out to fight the Midianites, a tribe of people who had been stealing the Israelite crops and leaving the people hungry. Once and for all he and his men must defeat these enemies or the Israelites would starve.

"If you win the battle with that many men, you will think your army did it without My help and will brag about it," the Lord said. "Send home the men who are afraid."

When Gideon told his army what the Lord said, 22,000 men went home. They did not have the courage to fight. There were only 10,000 left. "There are still too many," the Lord said. Then the Lord told Gideon how to keep only the very best. Gideon did exactly what the Lord said. He led his men down to a stream and told them to drink. Those who bent down and lapped the water like animals were sent home. They were not careful soldiers, for they could not see while they were drinking. Those who scooped water into their hands and looked around while they drank were kept. But there were only 300 of them. Those men had to have the courage to stay and fight with Gideon.

Gideon and his 300 listened carefully to the Lord. He told them what to do. In the middle of the night, they went up to a hill surrounding the enemy camp with trumpets, torches, and clay pitchers. They covered their torches with the pitchers, blew on the trumpets, broke the pitchers, and shouted. The enemy soldiers were completely surprised and thought they were outnumbered, so they began to fight each other. Each thought the others were Gideon's soldiers.

The 300 soldiers of Gideon could never brag that they had won the battle. The Lord had told them what to do. He had been with them and had helped them defeat a great army.

How did these men have so much courage? Because they trusted the Lord, they could do things the way He said. That's a good rule for us to remember, too.

JUDGES, CHAPTER 7

1. Gideon had this great army of _____ men. God reduced it to _____ (vs.3,6)
2. Why did God reduce the army so? _____ (vs. 2)

3. Who were they to fight? (vs.2) _____

4. The army was finally reduced to 300. By what method?_____
   _____ And, what did this mean? _____
   _____(See story.)

5. What did Gideon's soldiers take into battle? (vs.16)_

6. How did Gideon divide up his army? (vs.16) _____

7. Verse 20, Why did the soldiers break the pitchers? _____

8. How did the men defeat the Midianites? (vs. 19-22)

9. How were these 300 men able to defeat this huge Midianite army? (See story.)

10. Do you know why the Israelites were fighting these battles with the nations in this land?

BIBLE HEROES

SAMSON

A Story about Self-Control

MEMORY VERSE: Galatians 5:22-23 or Judges 13:24.

Judges 13

1. (Verse 2) There was a man named _____ whose wife was barren.
2. (Verse 3) What did the angel tell his wife? _____
3. (Verse 5) The angel also told them that the child was to be a N_____ that no _____ should come to his head, and that he would deliver Israel from the hands of the _____. *** These people were their enemies.
4. (Verse 24) The child's name was _____. As he grew the Lord _____ him.
5. Judges 16:6 tells one of his blessings. What was it? _____

Judges 14

6. (Verses 1-3) After Samson was grown, he went down to Timnah where he saw a woman who pleased him. He asked his parents to get her for his wife, and his parents were very disappointed. Why? _____
7. Although his parents were not happy about it they went down with Samson to arrange for the wedding. Verse 4 tells us that this was all part of _____ plan.
8. (Verses 5-6) On the way down to Timnah, Samson did something that showed his great strength. What was it? _____
9. (Verse 8) Samson met with his intended bride and his family made all the necessary arrangements for the wedding which would take place after a long wedding feast some days later. On his way back to the feast he noticed something unusual about the lion he had killed. What? _____
_____
10. (Verses 12-14) At the wedding feast he decided to make a riddle out of the strange thing he had seen. What was the riddle? _____
_____
How long did they have to solve the riddle? _____. What would be their prize if they solved it? _____
11. (Verse 15) After six days the men at the feast had not solved the riddle, so they went for

help from whom? _____

12. (Verses 17-18) No one had figured out the riddle, but Samson's wife had been crying and nagging him for seven days. Did Samson ever tell his wife? _____ Did she keep it a secret? _____

13. So who won the wager? _____

14. Did Samson know how they guessed? _____ Which verse shows that? _____

15. How did Samson pay his debt of 30 sets of clothes? _____

16. Was Samson happy with his new bride that he wanted so badly? _____ What was done with her? _____

Samson married a foreign woman—which was forbidden by God's law. She betrayed him. His bragging at the feast was showing off. He went against his parents will and put himself in a terrible position.

God was able to use both Samson's strengths and weaknesses to help the Israelites. He later used Samson's great strength to defeat the Philistines in a terrible tragic story.

Even though God tolerated the violent behavior described in these Old Testament stories, He never wanted man to behave in this way. In the new testament God shows us that we should live in a spirit love. Please try to learn Galations 5:22-23. It tells about the qualities a Christian should have.

JUDGES, Chapter 15 & 16

SAMSON
Part II

A Story About FAITHFULNESS

MEMORY VERSE: Galatians 5:22-23 (Surely you can get it in two weeks.)

Samson judged Israel and battled the Philistines for 20 years. Sometimes his weakness for women caused him to suffer, but his faithfulness to God finally gives him the victory over the Philistines.

Chapter 15

1. Samson used 300 _____ to set fire to the Philistines' _____. (vs. 4-5)
2. Samson used a _____ to kill _____ Philistines, (vs. 15)

Chapter 16

3. Samson used two very heavy _____ to escape from Gaza and defend himself against the Philistines who had surrounded the city and laid in wait for him all _____ (vs. 3)

4. Samson falls in love, again, with _____, and the lords of the city offered her _____ to find out where Samson got his strength, (vs. 4-5)

5. Verses 6-15 tell of three times Delilah ask Samson about his strength. What kind of answers did Samson give her on these three occasions?

   a. _____(verse 7)
   b. _____(verse 11)
   c. _____(verse 13)

6. Each time Delilah accused Samson of _____ her and she said that he didn't _____ her. (verse 15)

7. Did Delilah let it rest? _____ How did she treat Samson? _____(verse 16)

8. Finally, Samson tells all. Where was his power? _____ What would make him weak? _____(verse 17)

9. What did Delilah do? _____

   What about Samson's strength? _____(verses 18-19)

10. Without his strength, Samson was overpowered and they did something terrible to him. What was it? _____(verse 21)

11. Kept in prison, they used Samson as a grinder. They were happy that they had finally captured Samson and they called out to make him _____ for them. (vs. 21 & 25)

12. BUT, the Philistine guards failed to notice something important. What? _____ _____(verse 22)

SAMSON DID GIVE ONE LAST INCREDIBLE PERFORMANCE. Since he was blind, he had a young boy lead him around. He ask the lad to position him between the great pillars that supported the temple where the Philistine people had gathered to watch him.

13. Samson prayed for the _____ he would need to take vengeance on the Philistines (verse 28)

14. Tell what happened in these verses:
    a. verse 29 _____
    b. verse 30 _____

15. Did Samson try to save himself? _____,

So in his death, Samson killed more men than during his lifetime. More than 3,000 people died that day in the Philistine temple.

Samson had finally used his God-given strength to please God instead of himself. We all have some talent or blessing from God that we should use for God's glory. If you are strong, or smart, or athletic, or talented in some way, then you should try to use that blessing to do something for GOD. LET'S ALL TRY TO DO SOMETHING SPECIAL FOR GOD THIS WEEK.

BIBLE HEROES: The Book of Ruth

RUTH

A Story about Love

MEMORY VERSE: Ruth 1:16

The rain did not fall and the crops did not grow in Israel for a long time. Some people had to move away because there was no food. One family, Elimelech, Naomi and their two sons moved to Moab where the sons married Moabite girls, Ruth and Orpah. As time passed, Elimelech and his two sons died, leaving Naomi alone with these two girls.

One day Naomi decided to return to Israel where many of her people still worshipped God. The people in Moab did not do that. Orpah decided to stay in Moab with her friends, but Ruth went with Naomi. Together the two walked many miles to Bethlehem where Naomi once lived.

Ruth loved Naomi and tried to make her happy. Each day during harvest time Ruth went to the fields which a man named Boaz owned. There she followed the men who cut the stalks of grain and tied them into bundles. She picked up stalks of grain they had left behind and beat the grain from it.

"Who is that young woman?" Boaz asked his men one day. "That is Ruth," the men said. "She is the one who came from Moab with Naomi." Boaz wanted to talk with Ruth. "I have heard that you have been good to your mother-in-law Naomi," Boaz told her. "God will bless you for that." Then Boaz askd Ruth to come to his field each day to pick grain. "I will take care of you" he said.

God blessed Ruth because she was kind to Naomi, and because she had chosen God as her God. And God was happy that Ruth, Boaz and Naomi loved each other.

Ruth Chapter 1

1. Elimelech left _____ to go to Moab because of a _____ in the land. (vs. 1 -3) What is a famine? _____

2. At first, as Naomi and her two daughters-in-law started their journey back to Bethlehem, Naomi changed her mind. What did she tell the girls to do? (vs.8-9) _____

3. Verse 10 and 14 tell what the girls decided to do. What was it? _____
   _____

4. Verse 16 tells of a great love and devotion, from who to whom? _____,
   _____.

Chapter 2

5. There was a great land owner in Bethlehem. Name him _____

6. He was related to Naomi—how? _____

7. Verse 7 tells us about Ruth's work habits, write about them.

8. Ruth was surprised at Boaz's kindness since she was a _____ (vs. 10).

9. Why was Boaz so kind to Ruth? (vs. 11) _____

10. Ruth's kindness was repaid in abundance. Boaz directed his men to do something extra for Ruth in verse 16. What was it? _____

    How much did she glean that day? (vs. 17) _____

Chapter 3

11. Naomi is out to be a matchmaker!!! She thinks Ruth needs a husband to take care of her. In verse 3 she tells her what to do to attract Boaz attention. What was that? _____ (verse 1)

12. (Vs. 9) Boaz, being an honorable man knows that Ruth wants to _____ him. But, he also knows there is one _____ kinsman who must have first choice, (vs. 12-13)

Chapter 4

13. (Vs. 5) When Boaz approached the kinsman he tells him he must take _____ for a wife in order to buy _____'s land.

14. What did the kinsman say to this offer? _____ (vs. 6)

15. There was an action that validated a purchase or an agreement. When the kinsman did this he gave the okay for Boaz to have Ruth. What was it? (vs. 7-8) _____

16. So _____ and _____ were happily married (vs. 13) and God blessed them with a _____ and their neighbors named him _____. (vs. 17)

Naomi and Ruth were good women. Their qualities of goodness, caring, sharing and love were noticed by others. That is why Boaz became attracted to Ruth and wanted her for his wife. She may not have been a beautiful woman in looks, but her goodness radiated from inside and made her beautiful to him.

Ruth had come from a nation who worshipped "idol" gods, but Naomi had influenced her to turn to the Living God.

We can, through caring about others show them the way to Christ When we act right, are kind and considerate, people will see our Godly qualities and want to imitate those good qualities and learn to follow Jesus too!

Name _____ Date _____

BIBLE QUIZ

True or False:

_____ 1. Abraham was a Patriarch.

_____ 2. Joseph had two brothers.

_____ 3. Joseph had eleven brothers.

_____ 4. The Israelites crossed the Red Sea on dry ground.

_____ 5. Samson's strength was in his hands.

_____ 6. Ruth loved her mother-in-law.

_____ 7. Samson obeyed his parents.

_____ 8. Ruth loved Boaz.

_____ 9. Moses was an Egyptian.

_____ 10. A red string showed courage.

_____ 11. Gideon's army was many thousand.

_____ 12. Isaac was Abraham's son.

_____ 13. Abraham and Sarah were very young when their son Isaac was born.

_____ 14. Abraham was a man of great faith.

_____ 15. "Obey me and Jericho will be yours," God told Joshua.

_____ 16. Jacob's wife was Leah.

_____ 17. Jacob's wife was Rachel.

_____ 18. Isaac had twin sons.

_____ 19. Jacob's family went down to Egypt because of the mild climate there.

Match up these couples:

Abraham	Delilah
Adam	Eve
Jacob	Sarah
Isaac	Rachel
Samson	Zipporah
Moses	Ruth
Boaz	Rebecca

Fill In Blanks:

1. Joseph's father gave him a special gift, a _____.

2. Abraham loved God so much he was willing to offer _____ as a sacrifice.
3. Jacobs twin brother was _____.
4. The King of Egypt made slaves of the _____ people.
5. Baby _____ was hidden in the river among the _____.
6. _____ saw a burning bush. _____ spoke to him from this symbol.
7. Jacob worked _____ years for his beloved Rachel.
8. Joseph's _____ sold him as a _____ and he ended up in Egypt.
9. When Joseph was in prison he was put in _____ of the prisoners because he was _____.
10. There were _____ plagues brought upon the _____ because the Pharaoh would not let God's _____ go to worship.
11. Samson's famous riddle was about a _____ -
12. The great love story we have studied recently was between a mother-in-law, _____, and her daughter-in-law _____. They helped each other and took care of each other because they were alone; their husbands had ' _____.
13. "From the eater came something to eat. From the strong came something sweet." Who said this? _____ What was the answer to the riddle? _____ What was the sweet? _____
14. God promised Abraham, Isaac and Jacob a land flowing with _____ and _____.
15. Rahab showed courage when she hid the _____.
16. What sign did Rahab give to protect herself and her family when the Israelites took the city?_____
17. Gideon reduced his army to _____ men by sending home first those who were _____ then by keeping only those who drank water how? _____
18. March around _____ a day for _____ days and then _____ times on the _____ day. Blow the _____ and _____. When God's people did this the _____ of Jericho _____ down.
19. Samson regained his strength when his _____ began to _____ again.

20. _____ loved Ruth because she was so kind to _____ her mother-in-law.

21. _____ was the strongest man in the world.

22. Once Abraham was afraid of a King and pretended _____ was his sister.

23. What happened to the city of Sodom and Gomorah? _____
    Why? _____

24. Jacob and Esau were twins brothers. Who was the older? _____

25. Isaac's favorite son was _____. Jacob's favorite son was _____.

26. The Pharaoh asked _____ to interpret (or explain) his _____. He told him about a famine to last _____ years.

27. _____ was a great leader of the _____ nation. He lead them for _____ years through the _____ to the land _____ had promised them.

28. God sent plagues to prove his power to Pharaoh in asking him to let his people go. Three of the plagues were _____, _____ and _____.
    And the tenth plague was _____.

29. Match the person with a word best describing him.

    Joseph   Faith
    Moses   Trust
    Abraham   Patience
    Jacob   Love

30. Three great Patriarchs (Head of Families) were: _____
    _____ _____

31. How many spies did Rahab hide? _____

32. When Joshua and _____ spied out the land, they thought they could conquer the land with _____'s help. But the others said the people were _____ and were _____.

33. Samson _____ the lion with his bare _____.

34. What three things did Gideon's army carry when they defeated the Midianites?
    _____ _____ _____

35. Did the marching, or the shouting, or the trumpet blowing, or what...caused the walls of

Jericho to fall down? _____

36. If you could be one of the Bible characters we have been studying, which one would you like to have been? _____

I SAMUEL

SAMUEL

A Story about Reverence

MEMORY VERSE: I Samuel 2:26

BACKGROUND

Elkanah had two wives, Peninnah and Hannah. (At this time in history, God allowed polygamy—a man could have more than one wife.) Peninnah had children, but Hannah did not. Elkanah loved Hannah best and they were both sad because she was not able to bear children. Every year the Jewish families went to Shiloh where the tabernacle was to worship and offer sacrifices.

READ I SAMUEL 1:7-18

1. Why was Hannah so sad and for what did she pray? _____

2. Eli, the priest thought she was _____.

3. At the end of our reading Hannah was no longer sad, what had Eli promised her? _____

SAMUELS BIRTH AND BOYHOOD READ I SAMUEL 1:20-28; 2:18-21

4. Was God's promise through Eli fulfilled? _____ How? _____

5. Hannah had made a promise to God (I Sam. 1:11). In these verses you have just read, what did she do to fulfill her vow or promise? _____

6. Hannah made a gift for her little boy, Samuel. It was a _____ and she gave him this gift every _____.

7. How was Hannah and Elkanah blessed for their unselfish sharing of then son? _____

8. Chpt. 2:26 tells about Samuel's character. Explain what you think it means. _____

SAMUEL'S HONOR AND REVERENCE TO GOD

Samuel loved Eli so much. They had lived together for some time. Eli also loved Samuel like a son. Now Eli had two sons who were supposed to follow' in his priesthood footsteps but they were evil men. They would not listen when their father tried to correct their evil ways; and he allowed them to continue in their evil deeds.

READ I SAMUEL 3 (Read the whole chapter.)

9. One night as Samuel slept, something happened—what? _____
10. Who did Samuel think called him? _____
11. What did Eli say to Samuel? _____
12. How many times did this happen? _____
13. Finally Eli tells him it must be _____ wanting to talk to him. How was he to answer the voice when it called to him the next time? _____
14. God did speak to Samuel about Eli's family and his evil sons. In verse 12-13 he tells what he will do. _____
15. Samuel knew Eli would ask him about his vision. Did he want to tell about it? _____ Why? _____
16. Was Eli angry with Samuel? _____ What did Eli say about it? _____
17. What verse tells how Samuel continued in his work? _____
18. Everyone knew about Samuel. They all knew God made him a _____.

    Hannah took her promise to God very seriously. When we make a promise we should consider the responsibility of carrying through on our promise. It is a serious thing to promise ... and especially to God. <u>When we become Christians, we make a promise to God to honor Him and His Son, Jesus.</u> Do we cany this promise through as we should?

    We honor and reverence God when we attend worship services and when we read our Bible and when we pray. Also, we honor God when we tell our friends about Him.

JUDGES AND KINGS

Some of the men we have studied about were Judges ... Gideon, Samson .. and there was even a woman Judge of Israel—Deborah.

The time of Judges began back in Moses' time. As he judged the people's differences, his father-in-law Jethro advised him to get help. "Appoint good and honest men to help judge the people," Jethro told Moses.

There were many judges appointed during this period from the time of Moses to the time of the second king, King David. A time span of about 350 years. There were different types of Judges; some had more authority than others. Some served as Judges over a certain assigned area. Our Judges of today are similar as to judging over certain areas, authority, etc.

As Samuel became an old man, his sons became Judges. They were corrupt and the people told Samuel they wanted a King to replace his sons who were bad Judges.

"Give us a King like all the other nations have," they told Samuel and this was very upsetting to him. God told Samuel not to feel bad over this rejection, because the people weren't rejecting him . . . but were rejecting God.

God told Samuel to give them a King, but to warn them how it would be under a King. Their sons would be called to service in the army. They would be taxed a percent of their harvest and animals to support the King. Their daughters would be cooks and servants.

Still the people wanted a King. God allowed this to take place because of their lack of obedience to Him.

I SAMUEL

SAUL

Israel's First King

MEMORY VERSE: Found Within Your Lesson

"God has chosen you to be Israel's first king," Samuel said to Saul. Saul was surprised. He was a farmer, not a king. Only a few days ago he had left his father's home to search for some runaway donkeys. Someone thought the prophet Samuel could help him find the donkeys, so he came here to Samuel to ask. Now Samuel was telling Saul that he would be the king of Israel!

Samuel took a jar of perfumed olive oil and poured it over Saul's head. This was called anointing. It showed that God wanted the man to be king. "Let God be with you," Samuel said. "Do whatever you decide is best and He will not fail you."

Sometime later Samuel told the people of Israel to gather at Mizpeh. "You asked for a king," he said to them. "Now God has chosen a man named Saul to be your king." When Saul stood before the people, he was taller than anyone else in Israel. He certainly looked like he would make a good king.

READ I SAMUEL 9:1-2

1. Saul's father was _____.

2. Describe Saul from reading verse 2. _____

READ I SAMUEL 10:6-9

3. Samuel is talking to Saul. He tells him he will _____ and shall be a different _____.

4. He also tells him _____ is with him.

5. As Saul turned away from Samuel, he did have another _____. That meant God blessed him and was preparing him to be ruler of Israel—their King.

READ I SAMUEL 10:17-24

6. Samuel called the children of Israel together at _____.

7. He talked to them about their request for a _____.

8. As Samuel was about to present the chosen person for king, he had all the tribes of Israel pass by. When the tribe of Benjamin passed by someone was missing. Who? _____

9. When they looked for Saul, where did they find him? _____

10. What did the people say when Samuel presented Saul to them? _____

READ I SAMUEL 11:15

11. There was a great celebration at _____.

12. The celebration was the appointment of _____ as _____.

READ I SAMUEL 15 (Read entire chapter)

13. Saul was to take his army and destroy _____. Was he to spare anyone? _____ How do you know? _____

14. God told Samuel he was sorry he had made _____ the _____ because he would not _____ Him.

15. When Saul and Samuel met after the battle, what did Saul tell Samuel about the battle? _____

16. Samuel asked Saul about the noises he heard. What noises were there? _____

17. What excuse did Saul give for sparing the animals? _____

18. Samuel reminded Saul that he did _____ God and that was evil in the sight of the Lord.

19. Saul made other excuses such as _____ _____

20. Verse 22 stated God's instructions for obedience.
    "_____
    _____"

    THIS STATEMENT WILL BE YOUR MEMORY VERSE FOR THIS WEEK

21. Because of disobedience, Samuel told Saul, because he had rejected the word of the _____, He had rejected him from being _____.

22. As Samuel turned to leave, Saul grabbed his _____ and _____ it.

23. Samuel explained that the _____ would be _____ (torn) from Saul as he had torn his coat.

24. From this day on, even though Saul remained King for some time, _____ came no more to see him until the day of his _____.

25. Who was sorry he had made Saul king? _____

Even though he began as a good, concerned king, Saul failed to learn when to make good decisions. With God's help we can learn to make good decisions. If Saul had followed God's commandments, his family would have always remained the kings of Israel.

When we hear what God says, we need to exercise our choices of STOP and GO according to His will.

FROM JUDGES TO KINGS

A Review

1. God allowed _____ to appoint judges to help judge the Israelites.
2. Judges were over the people for about _____ years.
3. When the Israelites asked for a king, God told _____ to pick one out for them.
4. The first man to serve as king was _____. Tell three facts about him.
5. _____
6. _____
7. _____
8. He started his reign as a _____ king hut made many mistakes.
9. Samuel knew that God was displeased with _____
   I Samuel 16:1-3 tells what Samuel was to do.
   _____
   _____

DAVID IS CHOSEN: I SAMUEL 16

10. What happened in verse 10?_____
    verses 11-12?_____
11. Tell about David's family:
    a. His lather was _____
    b. He had _____ brothers.
    c. David was the _____
12. We know that David was a shepherd. Verse 18 tells 6 more things about David:

    _____   _____
    _____   _____
    _____   _____

13. Verses 16-13 tell why David came to live with Saul. _____
    _____
    _____

BIBLE HEROES

YOUNG DAVID

I SAMUEL, CHPT. 16-31

MEMORY VERSE. I SAMUEL 18:14

David was just a boy during most of King Saul's reign. David was an outdoorsman. He loved nature and taking care of his father's sheep. He was probably energetic and athletic, and he was also a poet and songwriter. He wrote many songs about God and nature. One of his most famous was the 23rd Psalm. Life for David was peaceful on his father's farm, but three of his older brothers were in King Saul's army fighting the Philistines, a strong and aggressive tribe of people who were killing many Israelites.

David was living with Saul, serving as his _____ (16:21) and playing the _____ for Saul when he ask (16:23). Saul and Saul's sons and daughters loved David and they treated him as one of the family, but David also spent time traveling back to his father's farm and carrying supplies to his brothers who were in battle.

I SAMUEL 17:4-12

1. _____ was the champion of the Philistine army.

2. He was _____ cubits tall (something around 9 feet.)

3. He had a helmet made of bronze, a coat of mail, _____ armor on his legs, a bronze _____ slung over his shoulder, and carried a very heavy _____. Every day he came out and taunted and dared the Israelite army and no one could defeat him. This went on for _____ days (v. 16).

When David would travel back and forth to the battle he saw the way the Philistines were doing the "armies of the living God" and he was extremely disappointed. Verses 32-51 tell about David and Goliath.

4. Summarize what happened:

   v. 32- _____

   v. 33- _____

v. 37- _____

v. 38-40- _____
_____

v. 44-45- _____
_____

What happened? _____
_____

I Samuel 18

5. When David and Saul's army came back into town they were greeted by joyous chanting women. What did they chant that made Saul angry? _____
_____(v. 7-8).

6. Saul's jealousy overcame him. Tell what happened in v. 10-14 and 28-30. _____
_____
_____

7. Why do you think Saul sent David into battle so often? _____

David did not hate Saul and he tried many times to convince Saul of his loyalty, but Saul was continually overcome by his jealousy of David and many times tried to have David killed. Saul's son Jonathan was a very good friend to David. Tell some of the things Jonathan did for David.

8. 18:3-4 _____

   19:2 _____

   19:4 _____

9. Someone else saved David's life in 19:11-16. Who? _____ How? _____
_____

10. Who was this woman to Saul? 18:20 _____

11. David was a renowned warrior which made many people around him either jealous or afraid. He spent a lot of time just trying to keep from being killed. Chpt 21:13 tells one way he saved himself from another enemy

12. _____ Saul remained a violent and jealous man for the rest of his life, there are some people who think Saul had some kind of sickness or disorder, but Saul eventually died a violent death in battle against the Philistines. You

83

can read about it in Chpt. 31 of I Samuel. Who else died with Saul? (31:6)
_____

13. A man who witnessed the aftermath of the battle reported to David. II Samuel 1:11-12, 17 tells how David responded to this news. What did he do? _____? In verse 19-27 is a song David sang in mourning for Jonathan and Saul.

2 SAMUEL 2—1 KINGS 2

KING DAVID

MEMORY VERSE: 2 SAM. 5:12 OR. 7:9

With Saul dead, the tribes of Israel were in turmoil. They were still fighting the Philistines but were also fighting among themselves. The Israelites became divided. *The tribe of Judah chose David to be their king,* but the other tribes had Saul's son Ishbosheth as king. The divided nation fought bitterly against one another. There were fierce battles, spies, schemes and assassinations.

Read 2 Samuel 4:5—2 Samuel 5:5

1. How did Ishbosheth die? _____

2. Was David pleased? _____

3. What did David become King of? _____

4. How long did he reign over Judah? _____ Over all Israel? _____

5. How long did he reign all together? _____

Read 2 Samuel 5:10, 12

6. David became greater and greater. Why? _____

After finally defeating the Philistines, David wanted to do more for God, so he built a special tent and prepared to bring the *Ark of the Covenant* to a place of honor in Jerusalem.

Read 2 Samuel 6:1-15

7. Tell about a man who lost his life while helping to move the Ark. _____
_____

8. After a 3 month delay, they tried to move the Ark again. Verse 13 tells how carefully they proceeded. _____
_____

The Philistines had been defeated, *the Ark was brought to Jerusalem* David had served the Lord faithfully. Israel was blessed with peace and David was living in splendor. David decided that he should build a fantastic temple to house the Ark and to worship God from, *but God had other plans.*

Read 2 Samuel 7:4-5, 12-13

9. What was the plan? _____

David was honored and thankful to the Lord for telling him that his son would be king and that his family would always reign over the Israelites. But David didn't know yet which son God would choose. David had several wives and many, many children.

10. How many sons are named at 2 Samuel 3:2-5? _____

11. How many were named at 2 Samuel 5:13-16? _____

2 Samuel 11 tells of a terrible sin committed by David.

12. Who did David become interested in? Vs. 2-3 _____

13. She was married to whom? Vs.3 _____

14. Uriah was a soldier. Vs. 14-17 tells what David did to Uriah. Summarize it: _____

_____

15. Did David get Uriah's wife? _____

16. Do you think David went unpunished for this sin? _____

Read 2 Samuel 12:1-7,14

17. Who pointed out David's sin? _____

18. How did he point it out? _____

19. How was David punished? _____

20. Vs. 13 tells us that *David repented of this sin and was forgiven.* He and Bathsheba had another son. Vs. 24 tells his name: _____

21. 1 Kings 2:10-12 tells what will become of this child: _____

_____

DAVID WAS CHOSEN OF GOD TO BE KING, HE LOVED GOD, BUT HE MADE A TERRIBLE MISTAKE. EVEN THOUGH WE LOVE GOD, WE TOO WILL MAKE MISTAKES. DAVID REPENTED OF HIS SIN AND ASK GOD'S FORGIVENESS. WHEN WE DO WRONG, WE MUST BE LIKE DAVID AND ASK GOD TO FORGIVE US.

DAVID HAD A GREAT INFLUENCE FOR GOD BECAUSE THE NATIONS AROUND HIM KNEW DAVID LOVED GOD AND GOD WAS WITH HIM. YOU ARE AN INFLUENCE FOR GOD IN YOUR NEIGHBORHOOD AND AT SCHOOL LIKE DAVID!!

RECAP OF OUR LESSONS ON DAVID

This lesson sheet is about David. It's also about the 2nd King of Israel.

David was just an ordinary shepherd boy who obeyed his father. He became famous when he met Goliath out where the Philistine Army and the Israelite Army had met for battle.

Did David take credit for killing Goliath with his sling and one stone? He told King Saul God would be with him as he had been when he protected himself from a bear and a Hon.

David had been taken into King Saul's palace to play his harp to soothe and entertain the King. David's best friend was one of the King's sons, and it was Jonathan.

As David became older he was a leader in the army and was so successful in battle that King Saul became jealous. There were songs sung by the people that made him furious with David.

The prophet Samuel had told Saul his sons would not follow him as King because of his disobedience, and Samuel had declared David to be the next King.

Let's take time to read the account of Saul who was king before David, and we can see why God was displeased with him. 1 Samuel 15:1-22, 24-28. There is also an interesting story between David and Saul—1 Samuel 24:1-12, 16-20

Saul and 3 of his sons died in a battle against the Philistines. One of Saul's remaining sons with some of his tribe declared him to be King—even as David was also made King by the tribe of Judah. God had not wanted a son of Saul to be King. Ishbosheth was killed and David was declared King of all Israel.

We have discussed David moving the Ark to a special tent in Jerusalem. Do you remember some details of this move? (We will discuss in class.)

Let's not forget that David is so well known and loved not only because he killed Goliath, but because he obeyed God. He made some mistakes in his life but was sorry and overall he loved and was loved by God.

I KINGS

SOLOMON BECOMES KING

MEMORY VERSE, Proverbs 22:1

King David had said his son would be king. *He was getting very old and was sick.*

One of his sons decided to make himself king. His name was Adonijah. He was not the son King David or God intended to be king.

While Adonijah was celebrating being king, King David had Zadok the priest and Nathan the prophet anoint his son *Solomon* to be king. When Adonijah heard this he was afraid and ran off and hid. Solomon was the son of David and Bathsheba. He was to be the third king of Israel.

READ 1 KINGS 2:2-4

1. David was about to die. He gave some advice to Solomon his son. List the things he said.

    a. _____
    b. _____
    c. _____
    d. _____
    e. _____
    f. _____

READ 1 KINGS 3:7-14

2. Solomon was concerned about being king; that he would be a *good* king. In this reading he talks about the Israelite nation being a _____ people, so large they could not be counted. Solomon asks _____ for an _____ heart so he could discern between _____ and _____. (He asks to be a wise ruler.)

3. God was _____ with Solomon's request. Because Solomon had not selfishly asked for _____, _____ and other things for himself, God gave him a _____ and _____ heart. He gave him more than he asked for, He gave him _____ and _____, and if he would _____ in God's _____ and keep His _____, he would have a _____ life.

READ 1 KINGS 3:16-28

4. Here we find a good example of Solomon's wisdom in judgment. Give a brief summary of

88

the problem. _____

_____

5. How did Solomon determine to solve this situation?
   _____
   _____

6. How did Solomon know the real mother?
   _____

READ 1 KINGS 4:29, 30, 34

7. God's gift to Solomon was so great, this gift of _____. From these verses make three statements describing this wisdom.

   a. _____
   b. _____
   _____

READ 1 KINGS 4:26-30, 34

8. Put into your own words Solomon's *wealth* and *wisdom* as described in these verses.
   _____
   _____

9. List the three kings of Israel up to this time, and out to the side of their name write if you think they were a good or a bad king.

   a. _____
   b. _____
   c. _____

10. Solomon's parents were _____ and _____.

NEXT WEEK ....We will learn about Solomon's building of the tabernacle.

WHEN SOLOMON WALKED IN GOD'S WAYS, HE WAS KNOWN EVERYWHERE AS A MAN OF HONOR AND WISDOM. A GOOD NAME IS WORTH MORE THAN RICHES.

1 KINGS

SOLOMON BUILDS THE TEMPLE

GATHERING MATERIALS

READ 1 KINGS 5 (Read the complete chapter)

1. Who is named in this reading as a great friend of Solomon's father, King David? _____ King of _____

2. *Why was Solomon to build the temple* and not his father David?
   _____
   _____

3. What two kinds of wood was King Hiram to furnish?
   a. _____
   b. _____

4. In vs. 6, Solomon tells about the laborers. Explain:
   _____
   _____

5. How were they to get the logs from Lebanon to the building site of the temple? _____
   _____

6. How did Solomon repay King Hiram? _____

7. How did Solomon divide his men's work time? _____
   _____

8. What other material was prepared for the temple? _____

9. Solomon was able to plan and carry out his mission to build the temple because of the _____ God had blessed him with.

BUILDING OF THE TEMPLE
READ 1 KINGS 6

10. Vs. 1. How long was Solomon king before he began to build the temple? _____

11. Vs. 3-5. How many *different parts* of the temple can you name from these verses?
    a. _____

       b. _____

       c. _____

       d. _____

       e. _____

       f. _____

       g. _____

12. Can you name any others? _____

13. This temple was *unique*, Vs. 7 tells us how. _____

14. What special thing was to be housed in the temple? Vs. 19 _____

15. What precious metal was used to cover the inside areas of the temple? Vs. 21-22. _____

16. Read vs. 38 and figure out how many years it took to build the temple. _____

THE ARK IS BROUGHT TO THE TEMPLE

READ 1 KINGS 8

17. Vs. 3-4. Who carried the Ark from Zion to Jerusalem? _____

18. Vs. 6. What was the place called where the priest placed the Ark? _____

19. Vs. 10-11 What happened? _____

20. What was the meaning of this? _____

READ 1 KINGS 4:20-31

Make a check here _____ when you have read it. We will discuss in class. If you read this and join in the discussion, it will count for your memory verse points.

1 KINGS

SOLOMON'S GREAT WEALTH

MEMORY VERSE: Know the first 18 Books of Old Testament

READ 1 KINGS 9:10-12

1. A *gift* was given but it did not *please* the receiver. What *gift was* given? _____
   Who gave the *gift?* _____ Who *received* it? _____

Verses 26-27

2. Name some riches of Solomon. _____

   READ 1 KINGS 10:1-7

   3. Who came to visit the King? _____
   4. What did she bring? _____
   5. Why did she come? _____
   6. Was she *impressed* with what she saw? _____
   7. What *profound statement* did she make? _____
   _____

READ 1 KINGS 11:1-8

8. Solomon changed in his actions. What changed him? _____
9. Who drew him away from God? _____
10. Had he been warned about this? _____ What verse tells us this? _____

Vs. 9-13

11. How did God react? _____
12. What was the punishment for this evil (sin)? _____
13. God made an exception because of his father David, what was it? _____
    _____

    God made an exception because of his father David, what was it? _____
    _____

Vs. 42

14. How long did Solomon reign? _____

Vs. 30—31

15. Who now became King? _____ of what? _____

92

16. Is this person Solomon's *son* or *servant*? _____ (vs. 26)

READ 1 KINGS 12:3-14

17. Rehoboam made a *decision* as King. What was it about? _____
_____

Vs. 23

18. Rehoboam was the son of _____ and ruled over the tribe of _____.

19. Based on his decision in question 9, *do you think he was a wise king?* _____

Because of Solomon's sin, the kingdom became divided. Jeroboam (the servant) became King of Israel (10 tribes) and Rehoboam (the son) became King of Judah (1 tribe.)

When Solomon obeyed God, he was blessed with untold riches and more wisdom than anyone had ever had before, but when he turned away from God, God did not allow his sins to go unpunished.

<u>The people had demanded a king. God had not approved, but had allowed them to have their king. When we turn from God and think we know more than He does, we will get into trouble just as the Israelite nation did.</u>

1 KINGS 17 -18

KING AHAB AND ELIJAH

MEMORY VERSE: Last 21 Books of Old Testament

"You are a *wicked man*" the prophet Elijah told King Ahab. "That is because you do not follow God. But God will show you how great He is. He will keep it from raining in Israel for a long time."

Ahab really was a wicked man. Since King Solomon died, many of Israel's kings would not follow God. Ahab was one of the worst. He prayed to idols of wood and stone. He even married Jezebel, a wicked woman who tried to kill those who worshipped God. But Elijah loved God and trusted Him to provide his needs.

Ahab was angry at Elijah for stopping the rain. He wanted to hurt Elijah. So God told Elijah to hide.

Elijah found a little si; earn by the desert, where he had water to drink and a place to sleep. Ahab would not find him there. But what would Elijah eat? Elijah knew when he saw a big black raven flying toward him, bringing bread and meat in its beak. Each day the raven brought bread and meat for Elijah to eat. God had sent the raven to provide for Elijah.

1 KINGS 17

1. Vs. 3. Where did Elijah hide? _____
2. What happened after a while that disturbed Elijah? (Vs. 7) _____
3. Vs. 9-11. Where did Elijah go? _____
    a. Whom did he meet? _____
    b. What did he ask her for? _____ and _____
4. Read Vs. 12-13. Explain in your own words these verses. _____
5. Vs. 14-16. Elijah told her not to worry. Why? _____
6. Who was responsible for what happened? _____

1 KINGS 18

7. Vs. 1. How many years since it had rained? _____
8. What did God tell Elijah to do? (Vs.1) _____
9. Vs. 2. What condition was in the land? _____

10. Vs. 5. King _____ and _____ were out searching for _____ for the _____ and _____.

11. Vs. 7-9. Elijah met _____ and told him to tell King _____ he wanted to see him. Obadiah was _____.

12. Vs. 16. _____ and _____ met.

13. Vs. 20-21. Ahab gathered his _____ and Elijah told the people they must choose between _____ and _____.

There was a contest between the prophet of Baal and God's prophet Elijah. They were to offer young bulls (bullocks) as a sacrifice except the fire was to be provided by Baal or God.

14. Vs. 25-29. What happened when the prophet of Baal offered their sacrifice? _____
_____

15. Elijah mocked them. How? (Vs. 27) _____
_____

16. Vs. 30-35. Elijah prepares for his sacrifice. He dug a _____ around the altar and then had _____ of _____ poured over the sacrifice.

17. Vs. 37-38. Elijah _____ to God and _____ came and consumed the _____, _____, _____, _____ and _____ up the water.

After this contest, Elijah told Ahab it would rain.

18. Vs. 43-44. How many times did they look toward the sea for signs of rain? _____

19. Vs. 45-46. _____ had to leave in his _____ in a hurry to escape the great rain that came.

20. Vs. 46. _____ gave Elijah great strength so that he outran Ahab's chariot and arrived at _____ first.

JUST THINK HOW GOD PROVIDED FOR ELIJAH AT THE STREAM.
- HOW HE PROVIDED FOR ELIJAH AT THE WIDOW'S HOME.
- HOW HE PROVIDED FOR ELIJAH AT THE CONTEST.

GOD PROVIDES OUR NEEDS AS HE DID ELIJAH. ELIJAH TRUSTED IN GOD AND WE MUST DEVELOP OUR TRUST IN GOD AS ELIJAH DID.

1 KINGS AND 2 KINGS

ELIJAH and ELISHA
PROPHETS OF GOD

MEMORY VERSE: GALATIANS 5:22

1 KINGS 19:16

1. God told Elijah to anoint _____ to take his place as a prophet.

2 KINGS, Chapter 2

2. Vs. 2-6. Elijah told Elisha to stay behind while he went to _____ and to the _____ River. But Elisha refused to leave him and went along each time.

3. Remember how in the past God had caused rivers and seas to part and his servants passed over on dry land? Tell what happened to Elijah and Elisha in Vs. 8. _____
_____

4. Vs. 9. Elisha was allowed to ask a special thing of Elijah. What was it? _____
_____

5. Vs. 1 & 11. Tell what happened to Elijah. Write a statement about it from these verses.
_____
_____

6. As Elisha took Elijah's place as the prophet of God, Vs. 15 tell us "The _____ of Elijah doth _____ on Elisha." Where did this take place? _____

2 KINGS, Chapter 4

7. Vs. 1-7. There was a woman who had a debt left by her dead husband. She did not know how to pay the creditors who were threatening to take her two sons as slaves. What did Elisha tell her to do? _____
_____

8. Vs. 8-11. A kind Shunemite woman did a special thing for Elisha because he was a man of God. What did she do? _____
_____

9. Vs. 14-16. Elisha wanted to do something for her in return. He asked _____ his servant about her. Gehazi said she had no _____.

10. Elisha promised the woman a _____. Was she *surprised*? _____

Doubtful? _____

Vs. 18-37. Read these verses. We will discuss them in class. Be sure to read them well so you understand what you are reading.

IN THE DAYS WHEN ELIJAH AND ELISHA LIVED, THERE WERE NO BIBLES TO READ. THE PROPHETS WALKED OVER ISRAEL TELLING PEOPLE HOW TO SERVE GOD. THE PEOPLE HAD TO WAIT UNTIL THE PROPHETS CAME TO HEAR WORDS FROM GOD. ISN'T IT WONDERFUL THAT WE CAN PICK UP OUR BIBLES AND READ GOD'S WORD ANYTIME WE WANT. ARE YOU APPRECIATIVE OF THIS BLESSING? DO YOU READ YOUR BIBLE OFTEN? DAILY?

2 KINGS, CHAPTER 5

NAAMAN

A Story of Humility

Naaman was a very important man, commander of Syria's mighty army. But Naaman had one problem. He was a leper, and there was no cure.

Naaman's little servant girl knew how he could get well. "Naaman can be healed if he goes to Israel and sees the great prophet," she said to his wife one day.

When Naaman heard about this prophet, he set out for Israel at once and went straight to the king. The king was frightened. "Am I God? How can I cure you?" he shouted. "Are you trying to start a fight with me?"

When the prophet Elisha heard about Naaman, he sent a message to the king. "Tell Naaman I am the man he wants to see." Naaman jumped into his chariot and hurried to Elisha's house. "This man will do some great thing to heal me," Naaman thought as he ran to the door. But Elisha didn't even come out to see Naaman. He sent his servant instead. The servant opened the door and told Naaman, "Elisha says to wash seven times in the Jordan River and you will be healed."

Naaman stamped his foot with anger. "An important man like me should not have to wash in that dirty river," Naaman said. Then he started home. But his servants stopped him. "You want to get well, don't you?" they asked. Naaman thought about it. He was being too proud. He should do almost anything to get well, even wash in a dirty river. When Naaman stopped being proud and obeyed God's prophet, he was healed!

1. 1 Look up *leprosy* in your dictionary and write the meaning. _____
   _____

2. (Vs. 1) _____ was a _____ in the king's army. He was a _____ man and had won many _____.

3. (Vs. 1) There was one thing wrong with Naaman. It was a disease of _____ and there was no cure.

4. (Vs. 2-4) Naaman had a _____ who had been captured and brought to _____. She had good news for Naaman and his wife. This terrible disease could be _____.

5. (Vs. 7-8) Naaman mistakenly contacted the _____ of Israel instead of the

_____. The king was _____, but _____ said, "Let him come to me."

6. (Vs. 9-12) Elisha told Naaman what to do to be cured. What was it? _____

7. Did Naaman want to do this? _____
   Why? _____

8. (Vs. 13-14) Naaman reconsidered and went to the _____ River and dipped _____ times.

9. (Vs. 15) Naaman remembered to be thankful. He said to Elisha, "Now I know there is no _____ in all the _____ but in Israel. (In other words, God was the true God.)

AND...ANOTHER PART OF THE STORY:

10. (Vs. 20) _____, Elisha's servant decided he would take some gifts that Naaman had offered to Elisha but Elisha had refused.

11. (Vs. 21) Gehazi _____ after _____ chariot.

12. (Vs. 23) What gifts did Naaman give him? _____ and _____.

13. (Vs. 24) What did Gehazi do with the gifts? _____

14. (Vs. 26-27) Elisha confronts Gehazi about what he did. Was Elisha pleased with Gehazi's actions? _____ Would you say Gehazi was dishonest? _____

15. What was his punishment for his selfishness and greed? _____

FROM THIS STORY WE LEARN THAT GOD CAN HELP US MORE WHEN WE ARE NOT *PROUD* AND LET HIM HELP US.

READ I PETER 5:6. WHAT WILL GOD DO FOR US WHEN WE ARE HUMBLE? _____

WRITE THIS VERSE AND LEARN IT FOR YOUR MEMORY WORK POINTS.

_____
_____
_____
_____

ACTS OF THE KINGS
AND CHRONICLES OF THE EVENTS OF THE ISRAELITE NATION

MEMORY VERSE: EZRA 7:10

The rest of the book of II Kings tells us about many kings, both of Judah and Israel (remember the kingdom was divided after Solomon's reign).

Some of the kings were good and some were bad in their relationship to God. Let's take a look at a few of them:

ISRAEL

	Name of King	Years Reigned	Good or Evil?
2 Kings 13:1-2	Jehoahaz		
2 Kings 15:8-9	Zechariah		
2 Kings 17:1-2	Hoshea		

JUDAH

	Name of King	Years Reigned	Good or Evil?
2 Kings 15:2-3	Azariah		
2 Kings 16:1-2	Ahaz		
2 Kings 18:1-3	Hezekiah (Read chapter 22:1-6 to see what unusual thing happened to him)		
2 Kings 22:1-2	Josiah (Something unusual about him when he became king)		

Because this great nation became involved in idol worship so many times and disobeyed God, he allowed them to be captured by foreigners. After a period of time they returned and rebuilt their land.

We have studied from the books of Genesis through II Kings. Next comes I and II Chronicles which recaps our previous study. For example:

1. Look at I Chronicles 2:1-2, remember how Jacob was also called _____ and

here lists his _____ sons.

2. Chpt. 11 of 1 Chronicles, Vs. 1-2. What two kings are named here? _____ and _____

3. Remember Uzzah and what happened to him? Look at 1 Chronicles 13:9-10. He _____ because he _____ the Ark.

4. 2 Chronicles 34:1 tells of the young king—King Josiah who was only _____ years old when he became king.

NEXT COMES THE BOOKS OF EZRA AND NEHEMIAH

<u>EZRA</u> was a great scribe (teacher of the law) and priest. He reminded the people of their sins and told them what they needed to do. In Chapter 10:12 the people had listened and replied to Ezra, "As you have _____ so we must _____."

<u>NEHEMIAH</u> was an outstanding leader as Abraham, Joseph and Moses were. The laws (Laws of Moses) were found and read to the people. Nehemiah and Ezra helped the people to realize they were still God's great nation.

THE LESSONS WE LEARN FROM OUR STUDY OF THE GREAT PATRIARCHS—ABRAHAM, ISAAC AND JACOB AND OTHERS—AND OUR STUDY OF THE KINGS HELPS US TO KNOW THAT GOD IS TRUE TO HIS WORD…THAT HE WILL NOT ACCEPT ANYTHING BUT OUR BEST. HE WILL FORGIVE US WHEN WE DO WRONG AND WILL HELP US TO DO OUR BEST IF WE WILL TRY.

AS WE GO THROUGH OUR STUDY OF THE BIBLE, YOU MAY FIND YOUR BIBLE HERO THAT YOU WILL LOOK FORWARD TO MEETING IN HEAVEN.

ESTHER

AN ORPHANED GIRL BECOMES QUEEN

There was a King named Ahasuerus whose wife was Queen Vashti. She was very beautiful. The Queen embarrassed the King by refusing to come when he called for her. She didn't come because the king wanted her to appear before his drunken friends at a banquet. So this King decided to look for another Queen.

In the search for a beautiful young woman, a young Jewish girl named Esther was brought before the King. He was pleased when he saw her and she became his Queen.

Esther had an Uncle named Mordecai who had raised her and loved her. He had brought her up in the Jewish religion.

One day Mordecai overheard two men talking about killing the King. He told Esther and she told the King. After this, the King was very friendly towards Mordecai.

After a while there was a man in the kingdom who became very important to the King. His name was Haman and everyone bowed down as he passed by. That is, everyone but Mordecai. This made Haman so angry and he wanted revenge. Knowing Mordecai was a Jew, Haman convinced the King that the Jews were planning evil against him. He got the King to sign a decree to destroy all Jewish people in a single day.

A QUEEN SAVES A NATION

Queen Esther heard of Mordecai and the Jewish people's plight She wanted to help. Now, even the Queen was not allowed to go before the King unless he invited her. She asked all her people to pray for her, then went into the King. He was pleased to see her and when she invited the King and Haman to a banquet they were happy to go. In fact, there were two banquets.

Meantime, the King was reminded of something—READ CHAPTER 6—read all of it.

When Queen Esther finally told the King what Haman had plotted for Mordecai and the Jewish people...and that she too was a Jew, the King became angry. In our questions for this week we will see what happened to Haman, Mordecai, Esther and the King.

CHAPTER 2

1. Vs. 7. Esther was an _____ as her parents had both died. She was raised by her

Uncle _____.

2. Vs. 17. How do you know the King was pleased with Esther? _____
_____

CHAPTER 4

3. Vs. 14. Esther was afraid to go into the King's presence, but Mordecai told her perhaps God had placed her in the palace for a reason. He said, "Yet who _____ whether you have come to the _____ for such as this."

CHAPTER 5

4. Vs. 11-14.-Haman tells his good fortune to his _____ and friends. But he still gets angry every time he sees _____ at the gate. His family tells him to build a _____ for Mordecai when the decree is carried out to kill all the Jews.

CHAPTER 6

5. When you read Chapter 6 you know the King is talking about rewarding _____ but Haman thinks he is the one the King wants to honor.

CHAPTER 7

6. Vs. 4. At the banquet Esther tells the King she and all her people are to be _____

7. Vs. 5-6. King Ahasuerus was upset and ask who would do such a thing. Esther answered, "It was _____"

8. Vs. 9-10. Haman's conspiracy turned on him. Instead of Mordecai being _____ on the gallows Haman had built, the King said, "Hang _____."

CHAPTER 8

9. Vs. 6. Esther was still worried about her people. Remember the decree of the King to _____ her people. The King wrote another decree and the people were not killed. Vs. 16 says the Jews had _____, joy and _____.

10. Vs. 15. Mordecai had been faithful to the King and was honored with robes of _____ and _____ and a _____ upon his head.

We never know what influence we have on other people's lives. As young people you have friends your age who see your daily actions, whether good or bad, and are influenced by them. Older people observe us—are we caring and courteous?

In our lifetime, we contact thousands of people. Esther saved a nation. Who could guess how many people we can influence for Jesus Christ by how we act and do each day.

Books of Poetry

Job

Psalms

Proverbs

Ecclesiastes

Song of Solomon

JOB

MEMORY VERSE: JOB 1:22

Chapter 1

1. Job lived in the land called _____. (Vs. 1)
2. Job had a large family: _____ sons and _____ daughters. (Vs. 2)
3. Read Vs. 3. Would you say Job was a wealthy man? _____
4. Job's family was a close family. Vs. 4 tells us his _____ and _____ feasted with him on special days.

God and Satan had a conversation. God talked about how his servant Job was a faithful and obedient servant. He was a good man and God had blessed him with many good things. Satan said Job was only faithful to God because of the riches he had. He ask God to let him tempt Job and He would see that Job wouldn't be faithful.

5. Vs. 11-12. God told Satan he could do what he wanted to Job except not to _____ a hand on his _____.
6. FIRST, Job's flocks were raided and stolen; they were his _____ and his _____. (Vs. 14-15)
7. NEXT, fire from Heaven burned up his _____. (Vs. 16)
8. THEN, the _____ were stolen. (Vs. 17)
9. FINALLY, after one servant and another reported these tragedies, the worst thing possible happened. What was it? (Vs. 18-19) _____
10. Read Vs. 20-22. Did Job turn against God? _____ In all this, Job _____ sin.

CHAPTER 2

Again God and Satan talked. When God told Satan there was none like Job who was faithful to Him even in his adversity, Satan said it was only because God had not allowed him to harm Job's person.

11. Vs. 6. God allowed Satan to do what he would to Job except to _____ his life.
12. Vs. 7 What happened to Job? _____
13. Job's wife wanted him to _____ God (Vs. 9)

14. In Vs. 10, Job told his wife she was _____. He said we take _____ from God; we must take bad when it comes too. In all this Job _____ sin.

15. There were three special friends of Job who came to see about him. They were _____, _____ and _____. (Vs. 11) They came to _____ and _____ with Job.

16. Vs. 13. Job's friends sat with him _____ days and _____ nights. They _____ not a word because his _____ was very great.

JOB
Part II

MEMORY VERSE: PSALMS 46:10

As we go on into our study of Job, we find the three special friends of Job, Eliphaz, Bildad and Zophar begin to talk and question Job.

Chapter 4: Eliphaz speaks:

1. You have helped those who _____ and strengthened the feeble _____ (Vs. 4)
2. Now it comes on you, and you are _____ and _____. (Vs. 5)
3. Vs. 7 Now you would not perish if you were _____.

Eliphaz tells Job he must have sinned or these things would not have happened to him.

Chapter 8: Bildad speaks:

4. Perhaps this happened because you _____ against God. (Vs. 4)
5. Vs. 5-6. If you (Job) would seek _____ and make your _____ (repentance); if you were _____ and _____, God would awake for you and _____ you.

Chapter 11: Zophar speaks:

6. Zophar tells Job to _____ his heart. (Vs. 13)
7. He tells Job to put _____ far away. (Vs. 14)
8. Then he said "Surely you could _____ up your _____ without spot and be _____ and not _____. (Vs. 15)

Zophar urges Job to repent as did Bildad.

Chapter 12: Job answers his friends

9. Job feels he is _____ by his friends. (Vs. 4)

Chapter 14

10. Job tells his friends (Vs. 1), "Man who is born of _____ is of a few days and full of _____

Chapter 16

11. Vs. 5. Job says if his friends were in trouble, he would speak words to _____ them and _____ them in their grief.

Chapter 27

12. Vs. 4. Job will not speak _____ or his tongue utter _____

13. Vs. 6. Job says, "My _____ I hold fast and will not _____

Through this book of 42 chapters, Job discusses his situation with his three friends. Also, he and God talk about God's greatness and Job acknowledges his lowness and dependency on God. It is a book that tells of great heartache and grief and pain for Job. BUT through it all—Job did not sin. THEN things changed for Job.

Chapter 42

14. Job tells God, "You can do _____." (Vs. 2)

15. Vs. 7. God tells _____ His wrath is against him and his two friends for they have not spoken that which is _____ to his servant _____.

16. Because of Job's faithfulness, God did some wonderful things for him.

    a. Vs. 12—He gave him _____ sheep, _____ camels, _____ oxen, _____ donkeys.

    b. Vs. 13—He had _____ sons and _____ daughters (Vs. 15 says his daughters were _____.)

17. Vs. 16. Job lived _____ more years and saw his _____ and grandchildren and _____ generations.

Probably none of us will ever have the tragedies Job suffered, but we will have some troubles in our lifetime. When we have sickness, sadness and sometimes loss of our loved ones, we should remember as did Job that God will be there for us in the end.

God is still in control of this world as He was in Job's time; *and He always will be.*

When you hear someone say a person has "the patience of Job," you will know whom they are referring to. Remember, through all of Jobs troubles, losses, friends turning on him...he sinned not.

PSALMS

David wrote most of the Psalms. The book of Psalms teaches us that God wants us to come to Him just as we are. He will strengthen us, help us solve our problems and deliver us to a good life. David asks for God's help, was sorry for his wrong doings, and gave joyful praise to God for helping him.

PSALM 23

1. David wrote this wonderful Psalm about God being our shepherd and caring for us. Read through it. It has only _____ verses.

2. First, David tells us who the shepherd is. _____ (Vs. 1)

3. In Vs. 1 he begins to tell us if we have God as our shepherd, we will not _____ for our daily needs, because…

4. Vs. 2-3 tells us God leads us beside _____ waters (peaceful, quiet places.) He _____ our soul (gives us strength). He helps us walk in paths of _____ (helps us to do what is right).

5. Vs. 4. We learn that even though we must walk through some dark valleys (sadness), we should _____ no _____ because God's rod and and staff (His words of love) will _____ us.

6. Vs. 5 Even in the presence of our _____ if we have some, He protects us if we are righteous.

7. Vs. 6 _____ and _____ will follow us every day and we will _____ in God's house forever (Heaven.)

PSALM 100

This Psalm is a song of praise and thanksgiving to God.

1. Vs. I Make a _____ noise (shout) to the Lord.

2. Vs. 2 _____ the Lord with gladness.

3. Vs. 3 _____ has made us and not we _____. We are His _____.

4. Vs. 4 Be _____ and _____ His name.

5. Vs. 5 For God (the Lord) is _____. is _____ and _____.

While reading the Psalms, have you noticed the endearing and majestic references David uses when talking to God. Look at Psalms 146-150. The beginning words of each are a praise to God. Throughout the book he refers to God as good, as an awesome God, as a caring God, in one reference, he states "hold thou me up and I shall be safe" and "thy word is a lamp unto my feet, and a light unto my path." What are the words that begin chapters 146-150?

"_____ _____ _____ _____"

CHAPTER 139

To your teacher this is a personal Psalm because as he speaks you know he knows all about David (and you) and cares for David (and you). First read the whole Psalm, then go back and fill in these few statements.

Vs. 2 Thou knowest my _____ and mine uprising, thou _____ my thoughts _____ _____.

Vs. 7 Whither shall I go from thy _____? Or whither shall I _____ from thy _____.

Vs. 14 I will praise thee; for I am _____ and _____ made: marvelous are thy _____

Vs 23 & 24. Search me O God, and _____ my heart: try me, and _____ me, and know my _____. And see if _____ ____ _____ _____ way in me, and _____ me in the way of everlasting.

This is a wonderful chapter in this marvelous book of Psalms. You will read and reread them all of your life and perhaps memorize many of them. In memory (memorizing) they will add much to your Bible knowledge.

PROVERBS

MEMORY VERSE: Proverbs 21:3

Proverbs is a book of instructions on how God wants us to live. Solomon wrote many of the proverbs along with other writers but the inspiration for these writings came from God.

If we trust God and have reverence for His word, we will have a good life. Not only does God give us these special instructions, but he **expects** us to use our common sense.

Proverbs has _____ chapters.

It is the __th book of the Old Testament.

Some of these instructions are in the following statements.

1. The beginning of wisdom is in _____ of the Lord (1:7).

2. Read 3:11 & 12. If God or your parent corrects you, it is because he _____ you.

3. (4:7) If you get wisdom you will also get _____

4. We know of a small insect that is busy all the time. God doesn't want us to be lazy, he wants us to be busy like the _____ (6:6).

5. Chapter 6:16-19 tells us 7 things the Lord hates. List them:

    a. _____
    b. _____
    c. _____
    d. _____
    e. _____
    f. _____
    g. _____

6. A _____ son makes a glad father, but a _____ son makes his mother _____ (10:1).

7. He that spareth the _____, _____ his son (13:24). Let's discuss this.

8. An angry person is _____, and a wicked person is _____ (14:17).

9. The wicked are an _____ to the Lord, but He loves those who

follow _____ (15:9).

10. It is important to have a good name. In 22:1 it says it is better than great _____. Let's discuss.

11. Boast not about yourself because _____ may change things (27:1)

12. Pride can bring you _____ but honor _____ you (29:23).

13. The last chapter, 31, is about a woman who is special because she is caring. It says in vs. 20 she helps the _____ and _____. In vs. 28 her children are _____ because of her care for them. Vs. 11 states her husband _____ her. Vs 26 says she speaks _____

The book of Proverbs is full of wise statements. If we study them and try to live according to their instructions, we will be caring, fair, honest and especially wise people. Most of all, we will be the people God wants us to be.

ECCLESIASTES

Ecclesiastes is in the "Books of Poetry" section of the Old Testament. It is a book which describes things we should not do. It shows us that living just to please ourselves without considering the needs of others is living a wasted life. The highest good in life is in obeying and respecting God and His ways of enjoying life.

The author is thought to be Solomon and notice the first verse of the book: "The words of the _____, the son of _____, King of Jerusalem." We know Solomon was the son of David and also that he was King.

How many chapters are in Ecclesiastes? _____ And, the book before it is _____ and after is _____. Remember, anytime you aren't sure just where one of the books of the Old Testament is, just use your Table of Contents.

Vanity and vexation are words used over and over in the book of Ecclesiastes. For example, look at Chapter 1:4-9 and then vs. 14. We will discuss in class, but look these words up in the dictionary.

Vanity _____

Vexation _____

Probably the most quoted scriptures from Ecclesiastes, and perhaps from the Old Testament, are found in Chapter 3:1-8. We will read these together in class. Read and fill in the blanks.

1. To everything there is a _____, and a _____ to every purpose under heaven.

2. A time to _____, and a time to _____; a time to _____, and a time to _____ that which is planted/

3. A time to _____, and a _____ to heal; a time to _____, and a time to _____.

4. A time to _____, and a time to laugh; a time to _____, a time to _____ and a time to _____;

5. A time to _____; and a time to _____ stones together; a _____ to embrace, and a time to refrain from embracing.

6. A time to _____, and a time to lose; a _____ to _____, and a time to cast away.

7. A time to rend, and a time to _____; a time to _____, and a _____ to speak.

8. A time to _____, and a time to _____; a _____ of _____, and a _____ of peace.

9. (Vs. 9:10) Whatsoever thy hand _____ to do, do it with thy might; for there is no work, nor device, nor _____, nor wisdom, in the _____.

Read 10:1- What do you think that means. We will discuss in class and also use a modern English translation to help us understand.

Also 11:4 and we will discuss in class. Read it

Read 12:13-14 and think about what you read. Jot down a thought or two if you can. We will discuss this in class also.

_____
_____
_____

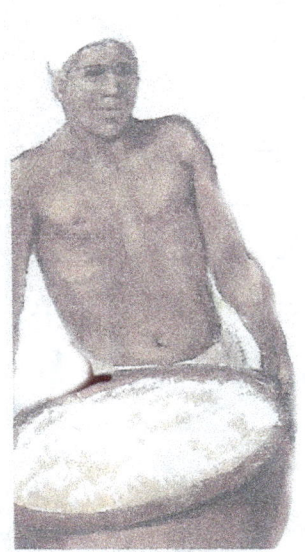

These are just a few thoughts on Ecclesiastes. There's a lot more to learn from reading and studying this book as well as any book of the Bible. Remember, they are God inspired for our learning and our ultimate goal of reaching Heaven.

MEMORY VERSE: Without looking at your paper, tell us 4 of the "a time to" statements.

SONG OF SOLOMON

SONG OF SONGS

MEMORY VERSE: I Kings 4:30

When Solomon was made King, remember God ask him what he would want, for He would give him whatever he ask; Solomon ask for an understanding heart to judge the people right. However, in his future reign, he disobeyed God. We studied about this when we were in the book of I Kings.

In this study, Song of Solomon, it is a poem or song written about the love that God wants a husband and wife to have for each other. As a couple prepares for marriage, marry and spend their life together, there will be times of difficulty, but they can overcome this and have a secure life through their deep love for each other.

THIS BOOK IS REFERRED TO AS A POEM, A LOVE STORY.

It is a very personal love story and better understood by adults. However there are words and phrases used that we might want to know about, so we will find their meaning in the list below. You might use your Bible concordance for some of these and also a dictionary.

1. Doves' eyes...1:15, 4:1, 5:12 _____
2. Roe and young hart 1:7, 2:17, 8:14 _____
3. Myrrh...5:5, 5:13 _____
4. Mandrakes... 7:13 _____

During our class time we will be reading some from this book. Since this lesson is short, concentrate also on your memory work.

For reading during class time,

2:1-13

4:1-4

6:5-10

Books of Prophecy

Isaiah	*Obadiah*
Jeremiah	*Jonah*
Lamentations	*Micah*
Ezekiel	*Nahum*
Daniel	*Habakkuk*
Hosea	*Zephaniah*
Joel	*Haggai*
Amos	*Zechariah*
	Malachi

PROPHETS OF THE BIBLE

There are *Major* and *Minor* Prophets in the Bible; the difference is in the length of the Book. The Major prophets are the ones who wrote the larger books.

MAJOR PROPHETS ARE:

    Isaiah

    Jeremiah

    Lamentations

    Ezekiel

    Daniel

MINOR PROPHETS ARE:

    Hosea

    Joel

    Amos

    Obadiah

    Jonah

    Micah

    Nahum

    Habakkuk

    Zephaniah

    Haggai

    Zechariah

    Malachi

WHAT DO YOU KNOW ABOUT A PROPHET?

What is a prophet? *A spokesman for God, a person chosen by God.*

Three typical tasks of a Biblical prophet.

- To hear the word of God.
- Tell the message of God.
- Be bold.

A Prophet's job: *To deliver a message from God to the people.*

> *To hear the word of God, to tell the people what God said and to warn the people to repent and pay heed to God.*

What is Bible prophecy? *The prediction of future events.*

> *Warnings when the people disobeyed God.*

THE OLD TESTAMENT PROPHETS- -

MAJOR PROPHETS	MINOR PROPHETS	
Isaiah	Hosea	Nahum
Jeremiah	Joel	Habakkuk
Ezekiel	Amos	Zephaniah
Daniel	Obadiah	Haggai
	Jonah	Zechariah
	Micah	Malachi

There were two prophets who did not die. Look at the scriptures below and see who they were...

Genesis 5:23-24 & Hebrews 11:5 _____

2 Kings 2:11 _____

What was the name of the prophet who parted the waters of the River Jordan?
2 Kings 2:13-14 _____

JEREMIAH is probably one of the greatest prophets of the Bible. He was called by God even before he was born to be a prophet. Read Jeremiah 1:4-10.

There are many prophecies concerning Christ from his birth even through His death upon the cross found in Isaiah. Following are some examples:

Isaiah 7:14 _____ fulfilled, Luke 1:31

Isaiah 53:7 _____ fulfilled, Mark 15:3-5

Here's one more Prophesy of Christ coming:

Deuteronomy 18:15, fulfilled John 1:45

Let's read it.

ISAIAH

MESSIANIC PROPHET

MEMORY WORK: Isaiah was the first of the Major Prophets. He was called the Messianic Prophet because of many prophecies concerning Jesus. His work as a prophet extended over 60 years.

Isaiah has 66 chapters and is in two parts. The first part covers 39 chapters and the second covers 27 chapters. It will be easy to remember this as it corresponds to the number of books in the Old and New Testament.

The prophet Isaiah was primarily called to prophesy to the Kingdom of Judah. Judah was going through times of revival and times of rebellion. Judah was threatened with destruction by Assyria and Egypt, but was spared because of God's mercy.

Some Key verses about his prophesy concerning Christ are listed next.

1. Isaiah 6:8 Then I heard the voice of the _____ saying, "Whom shall I _____? And who will _____? And I said, "Here am I. _____!"

2. Isaiah 7:14 Therefore the _____ himself will give you a _____: The virgin will be with _____ and will call him _____."

3. Isaiah 9:6 "For to us a _____ is born, to us a _____ is given, and the government will be on his _____. And he will be called _____ Counsellor, Mighty _____, Everlasting _____, Prince of _____."

4. Isaiah 53:5-6 But he was _____ for our transgressions, he was _____ for our iniquities; the punishment that brought us peace was upon _____, and by his _____ we are healed. We all like _____, have gone astray, each of us has _____ to his own way; and the _____ has laid on him the iniquity of us _____."

Do you know people who claim to be believers in Christ who are two-faced, who are hypocrites? That is perhaps the best summary of how Isaiah viewed the nation of Israel. In this book we see Isaiah challenging Israel (including Judah) to obey God with all their heart, not just on the outside.

ISAIAH'S DESIRE WAS THAT THEY TURN TO GOD
FOR FORGIVENESS AND HEALING.

JEREMIAH

MEMORY VERSE: Jeremiah 1:6

Jeremiah is the 24th book of the Bible, the second of the Major Prophets, and even though there has been discussion over some of the words and verses, Jeremiah is the author of this book.

After the death of King Josiah, the last righteous king, the nation of Judah had almost completely abandoned God. Jeremiah was warning them that God's judgment was at hand. It was painful for Jeremiah to have to deliver this message. Jeremiah loved Judah, but he loved God more. After further rebellion, God brought the Babylonian army back to destroy Judah and Jerusalem.

Jeremiah prayed for mercy for Judah as he trusted God to be good, just and righteous. We too must obey God, even when it is difficult, knowing that He will bring about the best for His children. And so, God promises the restoration.

1. (1:5) Before I _____ you in the _____ I knew you, and before you were _____ I _____ you; I have _____ you a _____ to the nations.

2. (7:30) For the sons of _____ have done that which is _____ in my _____, declares the Lord, they have set their _____ things in the house which is called by My _____, to defile it.

3. (17:9) The _____ is more _____ than all else and is _____ sick. Who can _____ it?

4. (22:9) Then they will _____, because they _____ the covenant of the _____ their God and _____ down to other _____ and served them.

5. (29:10-11) For thus says the _____, when seventy _____ have been completed for _____ I will visit you and _____ My good word to you, to _____ you back to this _____. For I know the _____ that I have for you, _____ the Lord, plans for _____ and not for calamity, to give you a _____ and a _____.

6. (51:56) For the _____ is coming against her, against _____, and her _____ _____ will be captured, their _____ are shattered. For the _____ is a God of _____, He will fully repay.

LAMENTATIONS

MEMORY VERSE: Chapter 3:41

This book does not absolutely identify the author as Jeremiah, but it is very likely that he was the author, as he witnessed the Babylonians destroying Jerusalem. Solomon's Temple, which had stood for about 400 years, was burned to the ground. Jeremiah was known as the "weeping prophet" for his deep caring and his having to watch all this destruction.

Lamentations 2:17. The Lord has done what He _____; He has accomplished His _____ which He _____ from days of old. He has thrown down without _____ and He has caused the enemy to rejoice over you.

The prophet Jeremiah seems to have written this book as a lament for what occurred to Judah and Jerusalem.

(3:22-23) The Lord's lovingkindnesses indeed never cease, for His _____ never fail. They are new every _____; great is your _____.

(3:40) Let us _____ and probe our ways, and let us and _____ to the Lord. We lift up our _____ and _____ toward _____ in heaven. We have transgressed and _____. You have not pardoned. (vs. 49) My eyes pour down _____, without stopping.

(5:19) You, O Lord, _____. Your _____ is from generation to _____

(5:21) Restore us to You, O _____, that _____ may be restored. Renew our _____ as of old.

Even in terrible judgment, God is a God of hope.

There are 5 chapters in Lamentations, each representing a poem.

EZEKIEL

MEMORY VERSE: Ezekiel 2:1-2

Ezekiel has 48 Chapters

Ezekiel is one of the Minor Prophets. His name means "God is strong." He was among the more than 3,000 Jews exiled to Babylon by Nebuchadnezzar and there among the exiles he received his call to become a prophet.

At about 30 years of age, he was determined as a priest/prophet called to minister to the exiles who were exceedingly sinful and thoroughly hopeless. He attempted to bring them to immediate repentance and confidence in the distant future.

He taught that God works through human messengers; that God can be worshipped anywhere; God's word never fails; people must obey God if they expect to receive blessings and God's kingdom will come.

Some key verses:

1. (2:3, 5) _____ of man, I am sending _____ to the _____ of _____, to a _____ people that has rebelled against _____; they and their _____ have transgressed _____ Me to this very day. As for them, _____ they listen or not—they will know that a _____ has been _____ them.

2. (18:4) For every _____ soul belongs to Me, the _____ as well as the _____. Both alike _____ to me. The soul who _____ is the one who will _____.

Have you noticed how many times you see this phrase "Son of man" in this book? Also this phrase "Thus they will know that I am the Lord." And, in the 37th chapter, he talks about dry bones. Perhaps in class you can read some of this prophesy and have a discussion on it.

Many dates are used in this book, in fact it contains more dates than any other Biblical book. Prophesies of this book can be dated more correctly by these dates shown.

3. (33:11) Say to them, "As I live _____ the Lord God, I take no pleasure in the _____ of the _____ but rather that the _____ turn from his _____ and live."

4. (48:35b) The _____ of the city from that _____ shall be "The

Lord Is There."

DANIEL

MEMORY VERSE: Daniel 6:22

Daniel was taken off to Babylon as a young boy. Although he was a young boy and a captive, he received an education and rose to a high position in the Babylonian and Persian governments.

Daniel and his three friends Shadrach, Meshach and Abednego were given special treatment in the royal palace as to the culture and language of the land. Also, a special diet was prepared that would make them strong. It was rich food that Daniel made up his mind not to eat, as did his friends. They talked to their attendant about it and he allowed them 10 days to see if they thrived on vegetables and water, which they did and appeared healthier. God gave these four young men special abilities for learning and to Daniel special abilities to understand meanings of visions and dreams.

This book shows us God's plan for ruling the world through human events, and the course of history and prophecies of future events.

The king of Babylon, King Nebuchadnezzar, had a dream that troubled him. He did not tell the dream, but expected someone among his magicians, conjurers or sorcerers to tell him his dream and interpret its meaning. They could not, so he threatened to have them killed when Daniel got word to the king that he could interpret the dream with God's help. The dream was as follows:

Chapter 2

1. The king's dream was about a _____ (vs. 31) that was large, great and awesome.
2. The _____ of the statue was of fine _____. (vs. 32).
3. Its breast and its arms were _____ and its belly and thigh of _____ (vs. 32).
4. The feet and toes were partly of _____ and partly of _____. (vs.33)

All of this had a meaning. When a stone was cut out without hands, it came and crushed the statue in its feet which being iron and clay stood for the kingdom of the Israelites which became a divided kingdom. Each part of the statue represented a part of the Kingdom of Israel that, having disobeyed God, fell and then became divided. After this interpretation, Daniel and his friends were promoted and given jobs of importance in the Babylonian kingdom. Now God would set up a kingdom which would never be destroyed, indicating through prophecy the kingdom of His dear Son Jesus Christ.

Daniel was a great prophet of God, and there is so much to study in this book, but we will touch on a couple more incidents and hopefully, as you grow in your knowledge of the Bible, you will read and study the whole book of Daniel.

Visualize this situation. In chapter 3 we read that the King set up a very large golden image for the people to worship. When the flute, bagpipe and other instruments of music played, the people were to _____ (vs. 6). The penalty for not doing this, which Daniel and his friends would not do, was to be thrown into a _____(vs. 11). But, as these young men knew, God would see to their needs, whether life or death. The furnace was so hot that the men chosen to throw them in were burned to death, but, as the king looked on, he saw men walking around inside the fire and then was convinced that their God had saved -them.

Chapter 4

5. Another dream of the King was of a great _____(vs. 10) The tree provided shade, food and also was a beautiful place for the _____ (vs. 12).

6. This tree was to be cut down with only a _____(vs. 23) left and since this great and powerful tree represented the King, he would be sent to the _____(vs. 25) to live with the animals for _____ periods of time (vs.25).

7. In verse 25 it tells why this is to happen to the king. He has failed to recognize _____'s greatness above himself.

8. In time, because the _____(vs. 26) was left, and if the king turned back from his sins to _____(vs. 27), his kingdom would be restored.

9. (Vs.34) After this period of time with the animals, the king _____ his eyes toward _____ and praised and honored Him who lives forever.

You have had class study through the years on Daniel in the lions' den. You will recall how God delivered him and the king who always seemed to follow his people when they tried to get rid of Daniel one way or another and then was sorry he made these laws and rules.

After being taken to Babylon, Daniel and his friends were given other names, they were: (Chpt. 1:7)

- Daniel _____
- Hananiah _____

- Mishael _____
- Azariah _____

129

HOSEA

Hosea is a minor prophet. His messages were intense and emotional and he was called "The Weeping Prophet" as was Jeremiah and sometimes Amos. He was a part of the Israel kingdom, the northern kingdom, and he labored through about 6 Kings so his work was over a longer period of time than some of the major prophets.

God told this prophet to go out and find a lady from the streets, a bad woman and marry her and have children. He is using this to show how Israel has left Him for other ways and how Israel has turned bad like this woman....and the things that will happen to her because of her disobedience.

Israel is in trouble. Just as Gomer has left home looking for other men and not respecting her husband...Israel has left God to seek false gods.

1. In chapter 3, (vs.4), God speaks to the people about their sin. "For the sons of _____ will remain for many days without king or prince. Without _____ or sacred pillar and without _____ or household idols, (vs. 5) Afterward the sons of _____ will return and seek the _____ their God and _____ their king, and they will come trembling to the Lord in the last days.

2. Chapter 4:6 "My people are _____ for lack of _____"

3. This statement will be your memory verse today. And the verse continues: "Since you have forgotten the law of your _____, I also will forget your _____."

4. Chapter 6:1-3 The people respond to God's rebuke. Read these verses and write what you think they want from God. _____
_____
_____

The Lord has compassion on His people. Chapter 13:1-3. Read these verses for discussion in class.

5. The more possessions the people had, the more idols they wanted. As they continued in their false worship, the prophet says, Chapter 14:1-2, "Return, O Israel, to the _____ your _____, for you have _____ because of your _____. Say to Him, take _____ with you and return to the _____. Say to Him "Take away all iniquity and _____ us _____."

Chapter 14:9. Here listed are the blessings that follow repentance. We will go over these in class. Be sure to read this final verse in this book of Hosea.

As you see in this lesson, the people were bad to leave God for false idols and other sins and He had Hosea marry a bad woman to show them their sin which we saw in the first part of this book. Gomer was the wife of Hosea.

Be sure to read all the verses indicated as we will spend time in discussion during class period.

JOEL

MEMORY VERSE: 2:18

Joel was a prophet of Judah and the first of a number of prophets to speak of Jehovah (God) to the southern kingdom (Judah). It was during his time that a natural calamity had fallen upon the area.

It was to a people hardened in sin that he spoke the judgment of Jehovah. It was at the time Judah was visited by plagues of locust that destroyed all vegetation and at the same time a drought occurred. In Chapter 1, vs. 2-3, he writes it was such a terrible thing that they should tell it to their _____, and their sons should tell it to their _____ in the next _____.

Joel declared to the people that it was a time for prayer and for fasting and for repentance.

Chapter 1

Vs. 1 The word of the Lord that came to Joel, the son of _____/

Vs. 4 What the locust has left, the _____ locust has eaten, and what the swarming locus has left, the _____ locust has eaten, and what the creeping locust has left, the _____ locust has eaten.

Vs. 18 How the beast _____! The herds of _____ wander aimlessly because there is no pasture for them. Even the _____ of sheep _____.

Vs.20 Even the beast of the field _____ for You; for the _____ brooks are _____ up.

Chapter 2

Vs. 12 Yet even now, declares the _____, return to Me with all your heart, and with _____, weeping and _____.

Vs. 14 Who knows whether He will not _____ and _____, and leave a blessing behind _____?

Vs. 18 Then the Lord will be _____ for His land and will have _____ on His people.

Vs.23 So rejoice, O sons of _____. And be glad in the _____ your God. For He has given you the _____ for your vindication. And He has _____ down for you the _____.

Chapter 3

Vs.20 But _____ will be inhabited _____ and _____ for all generations.

AMOS

MEMORY WORK: READ your lesson and then answer the question in the first paragraph and also in number 2.

Amos was not trained as a prophet nor was his father a prophet. He was a herdsman of sheep from a small town of Tekoa which was located about 6 miles south of Bethlehem. He was a native of Judah but was called by Jehovah to prophesy for Israel. (You remember from your other studies of the Bible that something important happened in Bethlehem—what?)

Even though Israel and Judah were having a peaceful and prosperous time, God was not pleased when he saw greed, anger and injustice among His people. Also, he could see that their worship had become just a matter of going through the motions. We need to be aware of our worship to God and be sure we do not fall into this type of worship. Amos' job was to warn the people so that they might change, however, they did not listen well to his teachings.

Amos was thought to be a great prophet and some think he was next in greatness to Isaiah and Jeremiah.

1. Can you look at the book of Amos and tell me how many chapters start with these words, "Hear this word that the Lord has spoken" or "Hear ye this word?" _____

   Amos has how many chapters? _____

2. (3:1) Hear this _____ which the _____ has spoken against you, sons of Israel, _____ the entire _____ which He brought up from the land of _____.
   (Remember when the Jewish people left Egypt—where were they going?)

3. (5:14) Seek _____ and not _____, that you may _____; and thus may the _____ of hosts be with

134

you, just as you have _____!

4. (7:10) Then _____ the priest of Bethel, sent _____ to _____ king of Israel, saying, _____ has conspired against you in the _____ of the house of Israel, the land is unable to _____ all his words.

5. (7:14) Then _____ replied to Amariah, "I am not a prophet, nor am I the son of a _____; for I am a herdsman and a grower of Sycamore _____.

Amos prophesied to Israel that they would be punished for their sins, however, he also tells them that God will allow them to be restored to their land.

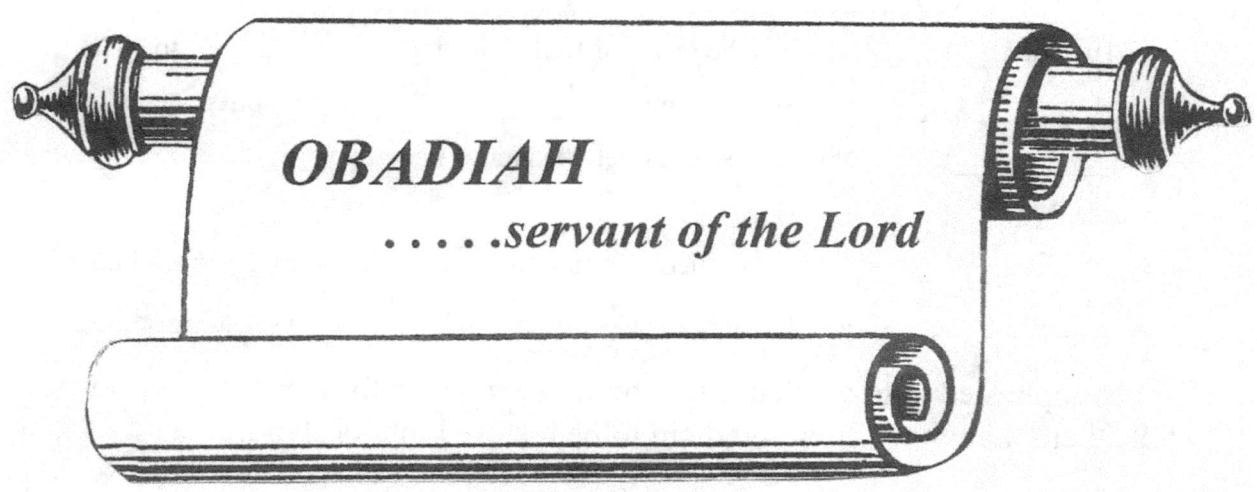

OBADIAH
.....servant of the Lord

This book of prophecy is only one chapter in our Bibles but is just as important for us to know something about its contents as any other part of the scriptures.

The prophecy centers around an ancient feud between Edom and Israel. You will remember how Jacob received the birthright that would have gone to Esau and this was over a bowl of porridge. The Edomites were descedants of Esau.

Write anything you remember about this occasion. If you do not recall anything, you might look at Genesis 27. _____
_____
_____

Vs. 10 Because of _____ to your brother _____, you will be covered with shame, and you will be _____ forever.

Vs. 15 For the _____ of the _____ draws near on all the _____. As you have _____, it will be _____ to you.

Vs. 21 The _____ will ascend _____ to judge the mountain of _____, and the _____ will be the _____

MEMORY WORK: Name 5 of the minor prophet books.

JONAH

All your life you have heard the story of Jonah and how he was swallowed up into the stomach of a "whale." But actually die scriptures say Jonah was swallowed up by a _____ the Lord had prepared (1:17).

1. The book of Jonah is a small book containing only _____ small chapters.

2. Jonah's call to preach to the city of _____ came from the _____ (1:2).

3. Jonah was foolish in thinking he could run away from the Lord, but he did run away and boarded a ship at _____ heading for _____.

4. We know that a great _____ (1:4) came and all the men on board the ship thought they would be lost and drown in the sea. They also thought this disaster was caused by sins of someone on board that ship. Everyone questioned their gods, as they worshipped pagan idols but the storm continued. Finally, they cast _____ (1:7) to see who might be the guilty party and _____ was the guilty one.

5. In verse 12 of chapter 1, Jonah admits he is guilty and tells them to _____ him into the _____. That is how Jonah got into the belly of that great _____

6. Jonah _____ to God; and in verses 9 and 10 of chapter 2, he is _____ for running away and states that _____ is of the _____. And _____ causes the fish to _____ Jonah upon the dry land.

7. In the first 4 verses of chapter 3, Jonah returns to _____ and preached to them telling them in _____ days _____ will be _____

8. Verse 5 of chapter 3 tells what the people did at Jonah's preaching. Fill in this blank with what they did. _____
_____
_____

9. In chapter 3, verse 10, _____ changed His mind and did not do what He planned to do, destroy them.

10. _____ was angry that the people had declared they were sorry. (4:1)

To continue our story of Jonah, and to know THE REST OF THE STORY, we will read chapter 4 in class and discuss it.

From this book of Jonah, and what it tells us about our relationship with God, we know we cannot hide from God, nor can we disobey his commandments. God knows everything about us, He knows if we want to please Him in living a good life and if we want to be in Heaven with Him someday. If we read our Bibles we will know what pleases Him and try to live that kind of life.

MICAH

VERSE TO REMEMBER Chapter 7:18

Micah was deeply sensitive to the social ills of his day, especially as they affected the small towns and villages of his homeland. His message went between that of doom and of hope. Micah stresses that God hates idolatry, injustice and rebellion, but he delights in pardoning the penitent.

Micah lived in the little town of Moresheth in the western part of Judah. Micah lived in Judah but he prophesied for Israel as well as Judah. During this time, while Israel seemed on a roller-coaster ride, ascending to the heights of its destiny in one generation only to fall into the doldrums in another, In Judah at this time, good kings and evil kings alternated with each other.

Micah was concerned so much over the treatment of the underprivileged that he called on God as their only source of salvation and mercy,

Micah's book provides a meaningful prophecy of Jesus birth and the world's future under the reign of the Prince of Peace.

Some verses to help us remember this minor prophet's writing:

1. (1:1-5) The _____ of the _____ which came to _____ of _____, which he saw concerning _____ and _____. _____, all of you; _____, O earth and all that are in it! and let the _____ be a _____ against you, The _____ from His _____. _____

   The _____ will melt under _____, and the _____ will be split.

2. (4:6-7) In that _____ declares the _____, I will _____ the _____. And _____ the _____, even those whom I have _____. I will _____ the _____ a _____ and the outcasts a strong _____. And the _____ will _____ over them in _____ from _____ on and forever.

3. (7:19-20) He will again have _____ on us; He will _____ our _____ under foot. Yes, You will _____ all their _____

into the depths of the _____. You will _____ give _____ to _____ and unchanging _____ to _____ which you _____ to our _____ from the days of old.

NAHUM

MEMORY VERSE: Chapter 1:7

Nahum is one of the Minor Prophets and came from Elkosh. Hebrew was his language. Little is known about Nahum and the place from where he came is not certain of location, some think near Jerusalem. But he writes that Nineveh is doomed because of murders, lies, treachery, and injustice. God rules over the earth, even over those who do not admit that he exists.

God determines where nations begin and end, and those nations that transgress His laws are doomed to destruction. However, a message of hope shines through. He offers good news to those who want blessings instead of judgment.

THE LORD'S ANGER AGAINST NINEVEH -

(1:1-8) The book of the _____ of Nahum, the Elkoshite. A jealous and _____ God is the Lord. The Lord is slow to _____ and great in _____. The Lord by no means will leave the _____ unpunished. Whirlwind and storms are His way and clouds are _____ beneath His feet. Mountains _____ because of Him and the _____ dissolve. And the rocks are broken up by _____. He knows those who take _____ in Him.

(1:14-15) I will cut off idol and _____ from the house of your gods. Behold on the _____ the feet of him who brings good news, who announces peace! Celebrate your _____, O Judah.

NINEVEH'S FALL-

(2:4-7) The _____ race madly in the _____. The _____ of the rivers are _____ and the palace is dissolved. She is _____. She is _____ away.

WOE TO NINEVEH -

(3:2-19) The noise of the _____. _____ horses, _____ flashing, _____ gleaming, _____ slain.

Nineveh is d _____.

Nahum, Habakkuk and Zephaniah were prophets during this time of destruction. Nineveh was the capital of Assyria. A prophet tells us what God is thinking and he tells us what God will do.

Nahum states that God still cares for those who trust him. Perhaps that is why he is called the prophet of comfort.

HABAKKUK

MEANING "TO EMBRACE"

MEMORY VERSE: Habakkuk 2:20

If you looked in your church hymnal you would find a song with this verse in it. "The Lord Is In His Holy Temple", "Keep Silence, Keep Silence, Keep Silence Before Him."

Habakkuk's name is mentioned twice in this book, each time with the title, the Prophet. He seemed to be a questioning prophet. He was of the tribe of Levi and possibly a temple musician.

Six lessons we can learn from Habakkuk:

1. It's okay to question God.
2. It is not for us to doubt that God has done or is doing the right thing
3. Never forget— "God is in total control."
4. No guarantees that bad things will not happen to good people.
5. We may be called to stand alone as was Habakkuk.
6. Learning to live by faith.

Read the following statement in 1:6, then note three things the Chaldeans might do from verses 7—11. _____

_____

_____

Read 2:1. Then fill in the blanks from vs. 2-3. Then the Lord _____ me and said, record the _____ and inscribe it on _____, that the one who _____ it may run. For the _____ is yet for the _____ time; it hastens toward the _____ and it will not fail. Though it _____, wait for it. For it will _____ come, it will not delay.

We are often downtrodden by our poor choices and our fallen world, however, the book of Habakkuk reminds us that no place is too dark and no wall too thick for God's grace to penetrate in a powerful and life affirming way.

ZEPHANIAH

"The Day of the Lord"

Memory Work: (End of lesson)

(1:1) The word of the Lord which came to _____ son of Cushi... in the days of _____ king of Judah.

The introduction of Zephaniah takes us back four generations, ending with Hezekiah, it is possible that this Hezekiah may have been King Hezekiah. Zephaniah was a young prophet and we know little about his personal life, but we do know that he was a prophet to Judah during the days of King Josiah.

The book of Zephaniah is probably best known for being the least known book of the entire Bible. It is a small book, located among the other Minor Prophets.

(1:4-6) Judah had embraced the idol of _____. I will cut off the remnant of _____ from this place, and those who had turned back from _____ the _____.

Through Zephaniah, God is predicting what will happen to Judah because of their disobedience. READ 1:7-18. What time does this remind you of according to other teachings of the Bible?

_____

_____

CHAPTER 2: *Judgment on Judah's Enemies*

(2:3) Seek the _____, all you humble of the _____, Who have carried out His _____; Seek _____, seek _____. Perhaps you will be _____ in the day of the Lord's anger.

(2:14) D_____ will be on the threshold.

(2:15) This is the exultant city which _____ securely, who says in her heart, I am and there is no one besides me. How she has become a _____.

In Zephaniah's writings he states that God's judgment for sin will be swift and severe, He also saves a remnant, thus-assuring Israel of their hope for the future.

CHAPTER 3:7, 8, 12, 14, 16

Read these verses... They each have some reference to deliverance which Zephaniah encouraged them to consider. We will have a brief discussion during class.

(3:12) But I will leave among _____ a _____ and lowly people, and they will take _____ in the _____ of the Lord.

Memory Work: Learn Minor Prophets:

Hosea

Joel

Amos

Obadiah

Jonah

Micah

Nahum

Habakkuk

Zephaniah

Haggai

Zechariah

Malachi

HAGGAI

MEMORY WORK: Haggai 1:7-8

The rebuilding of the temple is the center of interest around hich all that Haggai preached was involved. Little is known the background of his name. Since he was one who was left that remembered the temple in its former glory, he was probably 70-80 years old. Haggai was one of the first prophets which returned from exile to rebuild the temple. When Zechariah came back also, these two Prophets played a vital part in the rebuilding of the temple and the spiritual life of the Jews.

Some of Haggai's concerns about his work were:

1. The work had not been done. Now it was time to begin.
1. Everyone was concerned with their own house. While God's house remained in ruins, they were more concerned about their own houses.
2. The people were reproached for indifference.
3. Neglect in doing God's work had tainted their moral life, hence they had no desire to rebuild.

Some scriptures to look up:

1. (1:13) Then _____, the messenger of the _____, spoke by the commission of the _____ to the _____ saying, "I am with you, _____ the Lord."

2. (1:7) Thus says the _____ of _____, "Consider your _____! Go up to the _____, _____ wood and rebuild the _____ that I may be _____ with it and be _____," says the Lord.

3. (2:3) Who is _____ among you who _____ this temple in its _____ glory? And how do you _____ it now? Does it not seem to you like _____ in _____?

4. (2:9) The _____ glory of this _____ will be greater than the _____, says the _____ of _____, and in this _____ I will give _____ declares the Lord of _____.

5. Look at chapter 2, several verses in the middle of the chapter have similar wording, write down these words if you can find them.

   _____
   _____

Zechariah

MEMORY WORK: Psalms 22:27

Zechariah was not only a prophet but also a priest. He was among those who returned to Judah from their Babylonian captivity. Zechariah was the son of Iddo.

Zechariah was concerned about the rebuilding of the temple as was Haggai, but his time extended long after. He was also interested in their spiritual renewal.

There are many prophesies in this book concerning Jesus and his life on earth. We will touch upon a few of them in our question and answer part of the lesson.

1. (9:9b) Behold your _____ is coming to you; He is just and _____ with salvation. Humble, and _____ on a donkey, even on a _____, the _____ of a donkey.

2. (11:12b) So they _____ out 30 _____ of _____ as my wages.

3. (12:10). Read this verse several times and we will discuss in class.

While studying this, several references are made to Psalms 22. Let's also look at Vs. 1 and vs. 18.

MALACHI

The last book of the Old Testament is Malach. It is a short book with only 4 chapters. Malachi is considered one of the minor prophets and even though believed to be the last prophet, was around during some of the time of Ezra and Nehemiah.

Israel had been in exile in Babylon and was coming back home. God had allowed this exile time to try to bring the people away from idolatry and restore them to pure worship. They are back now and have restored the Temple, but the heathen nations are all about them and the prophets are reminding them of what they should be doing to please God and also looking forward to the coming of the Messiah.

Some of Malachi's statements seem rather harsh but he knows the people are neglecting the true worship and the Temple.

Chapter 1

(Vs. 2) I have loved you, saith the _____. Yet you say, "Wherein hast thou _____ us?

(Vs. 6) A _____ honoreth his father, and a _____ his master. And you say, wherein have we _____ thy name?

Chapter 2

(Vs. 10) Have we not all one _____? Hath not one God _____ us? Why do we deal _____ one with another?

Chapter 3

(Vs. 8) Will a man _____ God? Yet you have robbed me. But you say, "Wherein have we robbed _____? In _____ and in _____

(Vs. 16) A book of _____ was written before Him for them that _____ the Lord, and that _____ upon His name.

Chapter 4

Read the whole chapter. It is a short chapter, read it and we will discuss it more in class.

There is a long period of time between the close of Malachi and the beginning of the New Testament with the Gospel of Matthew.

The Old Testament is an introduction to the New. The understanding of the New Testament depends upon a like understanding of the Old.

The Old foretells the coming of the Messiah (Jesus), and the beginning of the New, the Gospels tell of his appearing.

FEAR, LOVE, OR BOTH?

FEAR: dread, terror, awe (reverent fear).

Are you ever afraid of your parents? Why?

To have fear for your parents does not mean they don't love you. To truly love them, to want to do the right things to please them, you must respect them. In Ephesians 6 there are instructions for both parents and children. Read vs. 4 and then vs. 1.

God is our Heavenly Father, do you ever fear Him? Why?

Fear of God just like fear for parents, makes us want to do what pleases Him. He provides us with everything we need to live in this world, all our daily needs. More importantly, He provides our spiritual needs — those things in us that make us want to do the right things—to be kind and good. But, just as our parents have rules, so does God. If we break the rules, we need to be afraid. The consequences of sin (breaking the rules) are terrible—so, we need to be afraid of displeasing God. He loved us so much He let His son die so we could have the good things... Heaven. We love God but we should fear Him and respect Him so we will choose to do right.

<u>Let's consider a few scriptures to see what the Bible says about fearing God.</u>

Ecclesiastes 12:13 . Then read vs. 14	Deuteronomy 4:10
Psalms 5:7	Hebrews 12:28
Proverbs 1:7	Psalms 115:11
Hebrews 10:31	Acts 9:31

1. Deuteronomy 6:5 "And thou shalt _____ the Lord thy God with all thine _____ and with _____ thy soul, and with all thy _____."
2. John 3:16 "For _____ so loved the _____ that he gave his only _____ Son that whosoever _____ in him should not perish but have _____ life."

FOR THE NEXT YEAR, I WILL TRY TO:

- ATTEND BIBLE CLASS REGULARLY.
- STUDY BIBLE LESSON EACH WEEK.
- LEARN MEMORY WORK WEEKLY.
- LEARN OLD TESTAMENT BOOKS.
- INVITE SOMEONE TO ATTEND BIBLE CLASS WITH ME.